MW01123166

Be Careful

God Has a
Substitute for You

In memory of
Dr. B. N. Olorunfemi
1952 - 2019
his love for Christ

Patrick Adewale Mould

ISBN 978-1-64492-606-2 (paperback)
ISBN 978-1-64492-608-6 (digital)

Christian Faith Publishing, Inc.
832 Park Avenue
Meadville, PA 16335
www.christianfaithpublishing.com

All Scriptures quoted are from King James version of the holy bible.

Printed in the United States of America

Other Books by the Author

1. I Called Abraham Alone-Getting Rid of Unfruitful Relationships
2. *What to Do When You Don't Know What to Do*

In memory of my late wife, Julie Otaniyuwa Mould (Nee Edionwe), who was to me and many around us then, a great general of God and a strong pillar to the ministry till God in His Sovereign wisdom recalled her home in April 2004 to join the Saints Triumphant.

When my present wife suggested the book be dedicated to her memory, I could not agree more, for she was indeed a rare gem and a gift to humanity. To live in the hearts of those that loved us is indeed not dying but living forever. Adieu, God's general.

Contents

Foreword

The message of this book is simple, scriptural, and practical. It is simple for everyone to understand that God is sovereign in His choice of instruments (human and material) in accomplishing His purposes in heaven and on earth. No one can hold Him to ransom. Though He has chosen men and women, none is indispensable before the Almighty. God often uses the weak and foolish things of this world to accomplish His purpose.

First Corinthians 1:27–29 says,

> Brothers, consider your calling; not many are wise from a human perspective, not many powerful, not many of noble birth instead God has chosen the world's foolish things to shame the wise, and God has chosen the world's weak things to shame the strong. God has chosen the world's insignificant and despised things—the things viewed as nothing—so He might bring to nothing the things that are viewed as something, so that no one can boast in His presence.

God has ready-made substitutes for anyone. I mean, anyone who disobeys Him or violates His principles. Let us be aware lest we become abandoned vessels. Sin is dangerous; let's avoid it at all cost. Let's not take our relationship with God for granted. The title of the book, *Be Careful,* says it all.

Pastor Patrick Mould, my friend and humble servant of God, amply demonstrates from the scripture how God had substituted many for various sins. It appears, in each case, the substitutes usually excelled in their given assignments more than their predecessors. We do well to remember Saul and David and Elijah and Elisha.

The book is practical. Each chapter has lessons for day-to-day living. For example, one of the lessons Pastor Mould draws from Eli's episode is that whenever God starts sending warning messages to His child or servant through a third party instead of talking to the person directly, it is time to tremble at God's word, repent, and run back to God without any further delay. The illustrations used by the author are insightful, helpful, and challenging. This book will be beneficial to all who will read, appropriate, and apply its message to life and ministry.

Cletus C. Orgu, PhD
Provost, LIFE Theological Seminary,
Ikorodu, Nigeria

Preface

I n my almost three decades in God's vineyard, I have seen many promising ministers of God (young and old) crash out of the race or turn into something else due to human frailties or carelessness with the calling of God upon their lives. Some failed and are still failing due to avoidable errors of the head that later took over their entire being and ministries.

Some started well, feared, and trembled at God's word, but through wrong associations or pressure to become big overnight without paying the price, have given Satan the chance to hit them with many poisonous arrows. A little compromise or disobedience here and there have become such a huge trap that they have been left wondering how the decay started.

In view of the fact that God's purposes are constant and eternal in nature, He does not change them; rather, He replaces any human being who refuses to diligently fulfill his or her own side of His eternal plans and purposes.

The Holy Spirit has therefore laid it on my heart to set forth the following pages to warn every child of God in general and His ministers in particular, so that they may not fall into the avoidable pitfalls that have consumed others before us in the ministry. God's work will not stop with you if you fail Him; He will simply turn His attention to another person to fulfill His eternal purpose(s), leaving you to continue your self-appointed "ministry."

God rejected King Saul and anointed young David as king while Saul was still alive sitting on the throne that heaven had turned into just a chair beneath him.

May God bless you as you read and put these solemn warnings before you, to guide your steps and decisions all the days of your life and ministries in Jesus's mighty name. You will not be replaced.

Acknowledgments

I thank God for giving me the privilege of putting His mind on paper through His inspirational insights. I am also highly indebted to the following great people for their various contributions to the writing and publication of this book.

My jewel of inestimable value, Pastor (Mrs.) Morolayo Mould, for her solid ministry support, prayers, encouragement, wise contributions, and proofreading efforts.

My beloved friend and partner in the ministry, Pastor Matthew Aisida, for his constant encouragement and support for this book.

My beloved brother, Samuel Idowu, and his wife, Mrs. Victoria Idowu, for the invaluable support and encouragement given to us over the years.

My seminary lecturer and Provost of Life Theological Seminary, Ikorodu, Nigeria, Rev. Dr. Cletus Orgu, for gracefully accepting to preview and write the foreword of this book in spite of his very tight schedule.

My beloved friend Apostle Paul O. Johnson who not only motivated me to write this book but also put in long hours and days of labor in designing the cover and the page setting of the entire book.

My beloved friend Rev. Emmanuel Dada Peter for his prayers, wise counsel, and encouragement in the kingdom work.

All members of Maranatha Royal Church for their prayers and constant support over the years.

May the good Lord reward you for your love, not only in this world, but also in eternity, in Jesus's name. Amen.

CHAPTER 1

God's Purposes and Programs

No sane man disputes the existence of God, the fact that He is the ultimate power having the final say over the affairs of heaven, earth, and all that are contained therein. He created all, and they exist or cease to exist at His pleasure,

> Thou art worthy, O Lord, to receive glory and honour and power: for thou hast created all things, and for thy pleasure they are and were created (Rev. 4:11).

> For by him were all things created, that are in heaven, and that are in earth, visible and invisible, whether they be thrones, or dominions, or principalities, or powers: all things were created by him, and for him. (Col. 1:16)

and He holds all things in balance by the word of His power.

> Who being the brightness of his glory, and the express image of his person, and upholding all things by the word of his power, when he had by himself purged our sins, sat down on the right hand of the Majesty on high. (Heb. 1:3)

God created the human race to occupy the earth for His purpose. He has His agenda for the human race in general and everyone in particular.

It is the responsibility of everyone to find out what is God's purpose for his/her life, surrender to God, and do all within his or her power to fulfill it.

God's programs and purposes have been set from eternity past and will continue to be carried out and fulfilled till we enter into the future eternity. God has always relied on men and women of all ages to execute His will on earth.

In order to fulfill God's agenda, He chooses people and equips them with power and all that is needed to play their own part in the larger program for the whole world. We must count ourselves highly favored to be so chosen. We must humble ourselves before God and mankind to fulfill these tasks without getting these funny ideas that God is relying absolutely on us alone and cannot achieve His purpose without us.

These ideas of self-importance always lead to chosen vessels getting into trouble and sometimes get them disqualified by God. God has a substitute candidate for every assignment He gives us if we disappoint Him or make ourselves either irrelevant or obstacles to progress.

God wastes no time in changing such individuals and giving marching orders to someone else to take over because His purpose cannot be defeated, neither can His word return to Him void.

> For as the heavens are higher than the earth, so are my ways higher than your ways, and my thoughts than your thoughts. For as the rain cometh down, and the snow from heaven, and returneth not thither, but watereth the earth, and maketh it bring forth and bud, that it may give seed to the sower, and bread to the eater: So shall my word be that goeth forth out of my mouth: it shall not return unto me void, but it shall accomplish that which I please, and it shall prosper in the thing whereto I sent it. (Isa. 55:9–11)

God may replace or change the vessels, but His plans and purposes, He does not change. Apart from the Lord Jesus Christ who has an absolute place in God's program for mankind because of His unique sacrifice and position, no one else is without a substitute. Everyone called and equipped by God for specific assignment must therefore humble himself/herself and carry out the duties with utmost sense of urgency, precision, and responsibility.

Pitfalls to Avoid

Usually, when God calls and equips someone for a divine purpose(s), such call and anointing attracts the attention of the devil and his hordes of demons. He becomes a marked man for attacks and manipulations (even while doing the work faithfully), but we thank God who also marks the person out for special protection by heavenly security. Hallelujah. However, along the way, we must be careful not to fall into any of the following avoidable pitfalls as a result of the subtle manipulations of the devil and his demons, capitalizing on human frailties in general and our weaknesses in particular. Otherwise, God will be compelled to replace us, no matter who we are or how big we think we have become in God's service.

1.   Toying with *or tolerant of sin*

On a general note, sin, no matter how small we may think it is, will compel God to call for our substitution if we don't repent within the timeframe God expects of us after warning us.

Sometimes we may not be involved in sin directly but condone people living in sin in our ministry because they are rich or our relations. If we keep them in sensitive positions despite this knowledge, God could be compelled to do a clinical cabinet reshuffle that may consume us. A case in point is that of Eli and his two sons, Hophni and Phinehas,

> And the messenger answered and said, Israel is fled before the Philistines, and there hath been also a great slaughter among the people, and thy two sons also, Hophni and Phinehas, are dead, and the ark of God is taken. And it came to pass, when he made mention of the ark of God, that he fell from off the seat backward by the side of the gate, and his neck brake, and he died: for he was an old man, and heavy. And he had judged Israel forty years. (1 Sam. 4:17–18)

whom God had to destroy in one day after their father failed to remove them from their sensitive positions despite warnings from God.

> And this shall be a sign unto thee, that shall come upon thy two sons, on Hophni and Phinehas; in one day they shall die both of them. (1 Sam. 2:34)

> And the LORD said to Samuel, Behold, I will do a thing in Israel, at which both the ears of every one that heareth it shall tingle. In that day I will perform against Eli all things which I have spoken concerning his house: when I begin, I will also make an end. For I have told him that I will judge his house for ever for the iniquity which he knoweth; because his sons made themselves vile, and he restrained them not. And therefore I have sworn unto the house of Eli, that the iniquity of Eli's house shall not be purged with sacrifice nor offering forever. And Samuel lay until the morning, and opened the doors of the house of the LORD. And Samuel feared to shew Eli the vision. (1 Sam. 3:11–15)

In spite of all the multiple adulteries and profanities of the sacrifices that his married children were indulging in, he kept them in office till God had to sweep his family clean out of the priesthood, replacing them with the young Samuel. What a sad end for a family that once had God's perpetual promise of priesthood office.

> And there came a man of God unto Eli, and said unto him, Thus saith the LORD, Did I plainly appear unto the house of thy father, when they were in Egypt in Pharaoh's house? And did I choose him out of all the tribes of

Israel to be my priest, to offer upon mine altar, to burn incense, to wear an ephod before me? and did I give unto the house of thy father all the offerings made by fire of the children of Israel? Wherefore kick ye at my sacrifice and at mine offering, which I have commanded in my habitation; and honourest thy sons above me, to make yourselves fat with the chiefest of all the offerings of Israel my people? Wherefore the LORD God of Israel saith, I said indeed that thy house, and the house of thy father, should walk before me forever: but now the LORD saith, Be it far from me; for them that honour me I will honour, and they that despise me shall be lightly esteemed. (1 Sam. 2:27–30)

Do not touch sin even with the longest pole, neither tolerate unrepentant sinners in your ministry cabinet or workship; the havoc can be very calamitous. Never ignore the first amber (yellow) warning lights from God; to wait till it turns red is to toy with one's eternity. No one should be too big to sacrifice in order to maintain your relationship with God and assure your blissful eternity.

2.   *Taking God for granted*

Sometimes, because of the great work God is using us to do and the level of intimacy with and revelations we get from Him, including the level of anointing He has gracefully bestowed on us, the devil may tempt us into becoming too familiar with Him as to begin to take Him for granted. We sometimes think God will always be with us no matter what we do and how we do His work.

2a. Not obeying God to precision—King Saul's example. Sometimes, we amend or modify the execution of God's instructions like Saul who partly obeyed God in destroying the Amalekites but sparing their King Agag, the beautiful women, and animals. He disappointed God so much that God told him, "To obey is better than sacrifice and to hearken than the fat of rams" (1 Sam. 15:22). In fact, God said disobedience is like the sin of witchcraft before him.

> And Samuel said, Hath the LORD as great delight in burnt offerings and sacrifices, as in obeying the voice of the LORD? Behold, to obey is better than sacrifice, and to hearken than the fat of rams. (1 Sam. 15:22)

2b. Samson Syndrome. Samson was a one-man army who lost out after his hair was shaven while sleeping on the lap of Delilah.

> And she made him sleep upon her knees; and she called for a man, and she caused him to shave off the seven locks of his head; and she began to afflict him, and his strength went from him. And she said, The Philistines be upon thee, Samson. And he awoke out of his sleep, and said, I will go out as at other times before, and shake myself. And he wist not that the LORD was departed from him. But the Philistines took him, and put out his eyes, and brought him down to Gaza, and bound him with fetters of brass; and he did grind in the prison house. (Judg. 16:19–21)

When the enemy came, he woke up and shook himself as before, but the Bible says, "He wist not that the Lord was departed from him" (Judg. 16:20). The rest is history; other judges took over because God will not allow a vacuum in His vineyard.

2c. Neglecting diligent seeking of God's face. Sometimes, we get so busy doing unnecessary things that we no longer have time for quality prayer, fasting, and study of God's word. We feel the anointing is still there. I have had some men of God tell me that they have done all their fasting in their early years of ministry that they don't need fasting anymore. I get alarmed because even our Lord Jesus Christ, after the initial forty days fasting, still fasted regularly throughout

His earthly ministry. One can easily enter into spiritual dryness if we fail to keep the fire fresh.

3. Pride

One of the things that God abhors most is pride; in fact, He said He knows the proud from afar off.

> Though the LORD be high, yet hath he respect unto the lowly: but the proud he knoweth afar off. (Ps. 138:6)

It was pride that led to the fall of Lucifer from his exalted position in heaven.

> How art thou fallen from heaven, O Lucifer, son of the morning! how art thou cut down to the ground, which didst weaken the nations! For thou hast said in thine heart, I will ascend into heaven, I will exalt my throne above the stars of God: I will sit also upon the mount of the congregation, in the sides of the north: I will ascend above the heights of the clouds; I will be like the most High. Yet thou shalt be brought down to hell, to the sides of the pit. (Isa. 14:12–15)

Pride, the Bible says, goeth before destruction: "Pride goeth before destruction, and an haughty spirit before a fall" (Prov. 16:18). When a servant of God gets to a point in service that he/she becomes entangled in the satanic web of pride, he or she becomes arrogant, boastful, impervious to correction(s) from others who know better. They hate the counsel of others because they think they know it all whereas the great Moses heeded the counsel of his father-in-law to delegate responsibilities which God worked with.

And it came to pass on the morrow, that Moses sat to judge the people: and the people stood by Moses from the morning unto the evening. And when Moses' father in law saw all that he did to the people, he said, What is this thing that thou doest to the people? why sittest thou thyself alone, and all the people stand by thee from morning unto even? And Moses said unto his father in law, Because the people come unto me to enquire of God: When they have a matter, they come unto me; and I judge between one and another, and I do make them know the statutes of God, and his laws. And Moses' father in law said unto him, The thing that thou doest is not good. Thou wilt surely wear away, both thou, and this people that is with thee: for this thing is, too heavy for thee; thou art not able to perform it thyself alone. Hearken now unto my voice, I will give thee counsel, and God shall be with thee: Be thou for the people to God-ward, that thou mayest bring the causes unto God: And thou shalt teach them ordinances and laws, and shalt shew them the way wherein they must walk, and the work that they must do. Moreover thou shalt provide out of all the people able men, such as fear God, men of truth, hating covetousness; and place such over them, to be rulers of thousands, and rulers of hundreds, rulers of fifties, and rulers of tens: And let them judge the people at all seasons: and it shall be, that every great matter they shall bring unto thee, but every small matter they shall judge: so shall it be easier for thyself, and they shall bear the burden with thee. If thou shalt do this thing, and God command thee so, then thou shalt be able to endure, and all this people shall also go to their place in peace. So

Moses hearkened to the voice of his father in law, and did all that he had said. And Moses chose able men out of all Israel, and made them heads over the people, rulers of thousands, rulers of hundreds, rulers of fifties, and rulers of tens. And they judged the people at all seasons: the hard causes they brought unto Moses, but every small matter they judged themselves. (Exod. 18:13–26)

I have sadly seen a General Overseer of a church who became a tin god to the point that everyone (male or female, no matter the age) who wants to talk to him must do so on his or her knees. When i noticed that he could not be corrected, I quickly conducted a dialogue with my legs, distanced myself from him before i become an accomplice after the act. If God spared not His Archangel Lucifer, don't even toy with any thought that He will spare anybody, including you.

4. *Love of money and fame*

When God starts using His servants, it is likely that financial blessing and fame may come their ways. It is important to take care not to start falling in love with money and fame to the point of personalizing the fame and the funds that come our way for the work of the ministry. We have seen some otherwise humble ministers of God who have suddenly personalized ministry funds and property to themselves and family members and assumed flashy lifestyles, seeking fame and commendation of men. They used many cunning methods to make members and non members part with their money and properties purportedly for God's work, only to realize that it has been turned into personal/family fortune.

The Bible says, "Seeketh thou great things for yourself? Seek them not" (Jer. 45:5).

Please watch out for this trap before God leaves you to manage your business empire while replacing you with another more faithful than you.

5. *Envy*

Many ministers of God have fallen into the satanic trap of dangerous envy and have destroyed their ministries and alienated those great people God sent to them to help accomplish their God-given tasks because they were envious of the gifts in the lives of those working with them.

These ministry gifts are given to ministers as the Spirit wills

> Now there are diversities of gifts, but the same Spirit. And there are differences of administrations, but the same Lord. And there are diversities of operations, but it is the same God which worketh all in all. But the manifestation of the Spirit is given to every man to profit withal. For to one is given by the Spirit the word of wisdom; to another the word of knowledge by the same Spirit; To another faith by the same Spirit; to another the gifts of healing by the same Spirit; To another the working of miracles; to another prophecy; to another discerning of spirits; to another divers kinds of tongues; to another the interpretation of tongues: But all these worketh that one and the selfsame Spirit, dividing to every man severally as he will. (1 Cor. 12:4–11)

to match their individual ministries, yet some, out of envy, have persecuted and frustrated even younger ministers under them with outstanding gifts because they felt those ministers will sooner or later become more popular and command more respect among followers/members.

A good example is the spirit of envy that moved King Saul to feel threatened by ordinary songs from women in praise of David who (though not a professional soldier) had just succeeded in killing Goliath, he had terrorized the whole Israel and blasphemed God openly for forty days. He said they ascribed one thousand to him and ten thousand to David, and they would soon give him the throne.

> And it came to pass as they came, when David was returned from the slaughter of the Philistine, that the women came out of all cities of Israel, singing and dancing, to meet king Saul, with tabrets, with joy, and with instruments of music. And the women answered one another as they played, and said, Saul hath slain his thousands, and David his ten thousands. And Saul was very wroth, and the saying displeased him; and he said, They have ascribed unto David ten thousands, and to me they have ascribed but thousands: and what can he have more but the kingdom? And Saul eyed David from that day and forward. (1 Sam. 18:6–9)

From that time, he started plotting how to kill David. Even when David was brought to drive the evil spirit tormenting Saul away, Saul still threw javelin at him. The rest is now history. It is sad to find a teacher or pastor envying the gifts or an evangelist or prophet in ministry.

Thank God for people like Moses who cautioned Joshua when he was shocked that Eldad and Medad were prophesying in the camp. (Although they were among the seventy chosen by Moses, they were not present during the ordination/anointing service, yet the Holy Spirit deemed it fit to rest on them where they were.) They felt they were intruding into the exclusive office of Moses and wanted Moses to stop them, but Moses told them he would be happy even if God made prophets of every leader.

> And Moses went out, and told the people the words of the LORD, and gathered the seventy men of the elders of the people, and set them round about the tabernacle. And the LORD came

down in a cloud, and spake unto him, and took of the spirit that was upon him, and gave it unto the seventy elders: and it came to pass, that, when the spirit rested upon them, they prophesied, and did not cease. But there remained two of the men in the camp, the name of the one was Eldad, and the name of the other Medad: and the spirit rested upon them; and they were of them that were written, but went not out unto the tabernacle: and they prophesied in the camp. And there ran a young man, and told Moses, and said, Eldad and Medad do prophesy in the camp. And Joshua the son of Nun, the servant of Moses, one of his young men, answered and said, my lord Moses, forbid them. And Moses said unto him, Enviest thou for my sake? Would God that all the LORD's people were prophets, and that the LORD would put his spirit upon them! (Num. 11:24–29)

I once conducted a weekday prayer meeting in 1986 at a branch of a popular Pentecostal church in Lagos where a young girl confessed to and was delivered of a spirit of witchcraft. The presiding pastor was fully briefed when he came on Sunday, and the young lady confirmed everything to him. I did not know he would become envious of me (because others having serious spiritual problems started opening up and asking for my prayers) until one day when I was away, he climbed on a table to announce that he is their pastor and not me, so they should not give me attention or ask for my prayers again. The members were shocked when I returned, and he "loudly and joyously" embraced me in a long time friendly manner. When I was briefed about his actions and open statements against me few days later, I knew it was time to quit before the relationship became more difficult. Do you know what? He did not even bother to visit me, let alone ask why I quit the church. We must never compare ourselves and our ministries with others. The apostle Paul said it is not wise.

> For we dare not make ourselves of the number, or compare ourselves with some that commend themselves: but they measuring themselves by themselves, and comparing themselves among themselves, are not wise. (2 Cor. 10:12)

6. *Using your privileged position to oppress others*

Sometimes, senior ministers use their privileged position to oppress other people. God is never happy with such ministers and may consider replacing them if they do not repent. Reflect on how Ahab used his position to seize Naboth's vineyard and killed the poor fellow because of covetousness.

> And it came to pass after these things, that Naboth the Jezreelite had a vineyard, which was in Jezreel, hard by the palace of Ahab king of Samaria. And Ahab spake unto Naboth, saying, give me thy vineyard, that I may have it for a garden of herbs, because it is near unto my house: and I will give thee for it a better vineyard than it; or, if it seems good to thee, I will give thee the worth of it in money. And Naboth said to Ahab, The LORD forbid it me, that I should give the inheritance of my fathers unto thee. And Ahab came into his house heavy and displeased because of the word which Naboth the Jezreelite had spoken to him: for he had said, I will not give thee the inheritance of my fathers. And he laid him down upon his bed, and turned away his face, - and would eat no bread. But Jezebel his wife came to him, and said unto him, Why is thy spirit so sad, that thou eatest no bread? And he said unto her,

Because I spake unto Naboth the Jezreelite, and said unto him, Give me thy vineyard for money; or else, if it please thee, I will give thee another vineyard for it: and he answered, I will not give thee my vineyard. And Jezebel his wife said unto him, Dost thou now govern the kingdom of Israel? arise, and eat bread, and let thine heart be merry: I will give thee the vineyard of Naboth the Jezreelite. So she wrote letters in Ahab's name, and sealed them with his seal, and sent the letters unto the elders and to the nobles that were in his city, dwelling with Naboth. And she wrote in the letters, saying, Proclaim a fast, and set Naboth on high among the people: And set two men, sons of Belial, before him, to bear witness against him, saying, Thou didst blaspheme God and the king. And then carry him out, and stone him, that he may die. And the men of his city, even the elders and the nobles who were the inhabitants in his city, did as Jezebel had sent unto them, and as it was written in the letters which she had sent unto them. They proclaimed a fast, and set Naboth on high among the people. And there came in two men, children of Belial, and sat before him: and the men of Belial witnessed against him, even against Naboth, in the presence of the people, saying, Naboth did blaspheme God and the king. Then they carried him forth out of the city, and stoned him with stones, that he died. Then they sent to Jezebel, saying, Naboth is stoned, and is dead. And it came to pass, when Jezebel heard that Naboth was stoned, and was dead, that Jezebel said to Ahab, Arise, take possession of the vineyard of Naboth the Jezreelite, which he refused to give thee for money: for Naboth is not alive, but dead. (1 Kings 21:1–15)

God had to deal with the whole household of Ahab for this evil.

> And it came to pass, when Ahab heard that Naboth
> was dead, that Ahab rose up to go down to the vine-
> yard of Naboth the Jezreelite, to take possession of
> it. And the word of the LORD came to Elijah the
> Tishbite, saying, Arise, go down to meet Ahab king
> of Israel, which is in Samaria: behold, he is in the
> vineyard of Naboth, whither he is gone down to
> possess it. And thou shalt speak unto him, saying,
> Thus saith the LORD, Hast thou killed, and also
> taken possession? And thou shalt speak unto him,
> saying, Thus saith the LORD, In the place where
> dogs licked the blood of Naboth shall dogs lick thy
> blood, even thine. And Ahab said to Elijah, Hast
> thou found me, O mine enemy? And he answered,
> I have found thee: because thou hast sold thyself to
> work evil in the sight of the LORD. Behold, I will
> bring evil upon thee, and will take away thy pos-
> terity, and will cut off from Ahab him that pisseth
> against the wall, and him that is shut up and left
> in Israel, And will make thine house like the house
> of Jeroboam the son of Nebat, and like the house
> of Baasha the son of Ahijah, for the provocation
> wherewith thou hast provoked me to anger, and
> made Israel to sin. And of Jezebel also spake the
> LORD, saying, The dogs shall eat Jezebel by the wall
> of Jezreel. Him that dieth of Ahab in the city the
> dogs shall eat; and him that dieth in the field shall
> the fowls of the air eat. (1 Kings 21:16–24)

David also used his position to impregnate Uriah's wife. When attempts to cover up failed, he ended up killing him indirectly.

> And it came to pass, after the year was expired,
> at the time when kings go forth to battle, that

David sent Joab, and his servants with him, and all Israel; and they destroyed the children of Ammon, and besieged Rabbah. But David tarried still at Jerusalem. And it came to pass in an eveningtide, that David arose from off his bed, and walked upon the roof of the king's house: and from the roof he saw a woman washing herself; and the woman was very beautiful to look upon. And David sent and enquired after the woman. And one said, Is not this Bathsheba, the daughter of Eliam, the wife of Uriah the Hittite? And David sent messengers, and took her; and she came in unto him, and he lay with her; for she was purified from her uncleanness: and she returned unto her house. And the woman conceived, and sent and told David, and said, I am with child. And David sent to Joab, saying Send me Uriah the Hittite. And Joab sent Uriah to David. And when Uriah was come unto him, David demanded of him how Joab did, and how the people did, and how the war prospered. And David said to Uriah, Go down to thy house, and wash thy feet. And Uriah departed out of the king's house, and there followed him a mess of meat from the king. But Uriah slept at the door of the king's house with all the servants of his lord, and went not down to his house. And when they had told David, saying, Uriah went not down unto his house, David said unto Uriah, Camest thou not from thy journey? why then didst thou not go down unto thine house? And Uriah said unto David, The ark, and Israel, and Judah, abide in tents; and my lord Joab, and the servants of my lord, are encamped in the open fields; shall I then go into mine house, to eat and to drink, and to lie with my wife? as thou livest, and as thy soul liveth, I will not do this thing. And David said to Uriah, Tarry here today also, and tomorrow I will let thee depart. So Uriah abode in Jerusalem that day, and the morrow. And when David had called him, he did eat and drink before him; and he made him drunk: and at even he went out to lie on his bed with the servants of his lord, but went not down to his house. And it came to pass in the morning, that David wrote a letter to Joab, and sent it by the hand of Uriah. And he wrote in the letter, saying, Set ye Uriah in the forefront of the hottest battle, and retire ye from him, that he may be smitten, and die. And it came to pass, when Joab observed the city, that he assigned Uriah unto a place where he knew that valiant men were. And the men of the city went out, and fought with Joab: and there fell some of the people of the servants of David; and Uriah the Hittite died also. (2 Sam. 11:1–17)

God got angry and sent Prophet Nathan to tell David that when he was a nobody in his own eyes, He gave him the throne and many things, yet he oppressed the poor fellow unjustly.

And Nathan said to David, Thou art the man. Thus saith the LORD God of Israel, I anointed thee king over Israel, and I delivered thee out of the hand of Saul; And I gave thee thy master's house, and thy master's wives into thy bosom, and gave thee the house of Israel and of Judah; and if that had been too little, I would moreover have given unto thee such and such things. Wherefore hast thou despised the commandment of the LORD, to do evil in his sight? thou hast killed Uriah the Hittite with the sword, and hast taken his wife to be thy wife, and hast slain

him with the sword of the children of Ammon.
Now therefore the sword shall never depart from
thine house; because thou hast despised me, and
hast taken the wife of Uriah the Hittite to be thy
wife. (2 Sam. 12:7–10)

You may not have slept with your members' wives, but how about the starvation wages you pay your full-time ministry workers, telling them, "Wait for your time" while cornering all the rest to satisfy your lust for luxuries?

Why do you think God will be happy when you post those who have planted good branch churches to remote areas either as unjust punitive measures or to make room for your sycophants or relations to go and reap others' years of hard labor? What of those who curse any church member who dares to assist or associate with ministers who have served under them faithfully for many years, simply because they are leaving to start a new ministry, even when they have not done anything to harm the ministry they are leaving? Remember how God intervened for Jacob after many tricks of Laban? God is still the same just God.

7. *Unnecessary haste*

In an unnecessary hurry to get the so called "breakthrough" in ministry, many have dabbled into the occult to attract crowds, wealth, or "miraculous power." This is a big trap the devil has used over and over to destroy ministers. One of the fruits of the Spirit is patience, yet most are in a hurry for "results." Our Lord Jesus Christ spent the first thirty years of His life preparing for ministry. Within about three years, He had accomplished His heavenly Father's mandate.

Why are you in such a hurry? If you are sure of your calling, stay within it and obey God's own blueprint for your task. You will get there. Can you imagine how many years it took Noah to finish the construction of the great ship? Yet he did it to specification despite the shame and ridicule his generation subjected him to.

Make thee an ark of gopher wood; rooms shalt thou make in the ark, and shalt pitch it within and without with pitch. And this is the fashion which thou shalt make it of: The length of the ark shall be three hundred cubits, the breadth of it fifty cubits, and the height of it thirty cubits. A window shalt thou make to the ark, and in a cubit shalt thou finish it above; and the door of the ark shalt thou set in the side thereof; with lower, second, and third stories shalt thou make it. Thus did Noah; according to all that God commanded him, so did he. (Gen. 6:14–16, 22)

Don't jump the gun, never use ungodly methods or means for God's assignments; it doesn't work that way. God gives everyone who is called the *wherewithal* to succeed. Yours can't be an exception. Don't embrace Satanism; you can only have sorrowful regrets in the end. God's work will continue without you, yes, without you.

8. *Grumbling and abandoning ministry because of hardship or fear of death*

Many ministers with great potentials have grumbled and abandoned ministry because of hardship (financial and otherwise) or the dangers that go with the calling. God wants His servants to serve Him cheerfully, no matter the cost even if it results in death. It is normal to experience financial hardship or lack in ministry. Remember: our Lord Jesus Christ was hungry after fasting for forty days and nights,

Then was Jesus led up of the Spirit into the wilderness to be tempted of the devil. And when he had fasted forty days and forty nights, he was afterward an hungred. (Matt. 4:1–2)

34

yet He did not succumb to the temptation of turning stone into bread at the command or suggestion of the devil.

> And when the tempter came to him, he said, If thou be the Son of God, command that these stones be made bread. But he answered and said, It is written, Man shall not live by bread alone, but by every word that proceedeth out of the mouth of God. (Matt. 4:3–4)

He also had to produce money from a fish to pay tax.

> And when they were come to Capernaum, they that received tribute money came to Peter, and said, Doth not your master pay tribute? He saith, Yes. And when he was come into the house, Jesus prevented him, saying, What thinkest thou, Simon? of whom do the kings of the earth take custom or tribute? of their own children, or of strangers? Peter saith unto him, Of strangers. Jesus saith unto him, Then are the children free. Notwithstanding, lest we should offend them, go thou to the sea, and cast an hook, and take up the fish that first cometh up; and when thou hast opened his mouth, thou shalt find a piece of money: that take, and give unto them for me and thee. (Matt. 17:24–27)

Can we be greater than our Master? Elijah had to be fed by angels and a widow at some points in ministry.

> And the word of the LORD came unto him, saying, Arise, get thee to Zarephath, which belongeth to Zidon, and dwell there: behold, I have commanded a widow woman there to sustain thee. (1 Kings 17:8–9)

And as he lay and slept under a juniper tree, behold, then an angel touched him, and said unto him, Arise and eat. And he looked, and, behold, there was a cake baken on the coals, and a cruse of water at his head. And he did eat and drink, and laid him down again. And the angel of the LORD came again the second time, and touched him, and said, Arise and eat; because the journey is too great for thee. And he arose, and did eat and drink, and went in the strength of that meat forty days and forty nights unto Horeb the mount of God. (1 Kings 19:5–8)

Let us adopt the Pauline position in:

Who shall separate us from the love of Christ? shall tribulation, or distress, or persecution, or famine, or nakedness, or peril, or sword? As it is written, For thy sake we are killed all the day long; we are accounted as sheep for the slaughter. Nay, in all these things we are more than conquerors through him that loved us. For I am persuaded, that neither death, nor life, nor angels, nor principalities, nor powers, nor things present, nor things to come, Nor height, nor depth, nor any other creature, shall be able to separate us from the love of God, which is in Christ Jesus our Lord. (Rom. 8:35–39)

Nothing should be able to separate us from the love of God. Some ministers run away from deliverance cases because they think they will come under satanic attack. I wonder whether they have read all the great promises of the Bible concerning our assured protection from satanic powers, such as:

Then he called his twelve disciples together, and gave them power and authority over all devils, and to cure diseases. And he sent them to preach the kingdom of God, and to heal the sick. (Luke 9:1–2)

And the seventy returned again with joy, saying, Lord, even the devils are subject unto us through thy name. And he said unto them, 1 beheld Satan as lightning fall from heaven; Behold, I give unto you power to tread on serpents and scorpions, and over all the power of the enemy: and nothing shall by any means hurt you. (Luke 10:17–19)

Behold, they shall surely gather together, but not by me: whosoever shall gather together against thee shall fall for thy sake. Behold, I have created the smith that bloweth the coals in the fire, and that bringeth forth an instrument for his work; and I have created the waster to destroy. No weapon that is formed against thee shall prosper; and every tongue that shall rise against thee in judgment thou shalt condemn. This is the heritage of the servants of the LORD, and their righteousness is of me, saith the LORD. (Isa. 54:15–17)

and many more. Jesus Christ dealt with healing and deliverance cases without fear and has ordered us to do the same. Our lives are in the hands of God. Nobody can take it without God's knowledge and permission. We should not be afraid to confront the hordes of hell headlong, knowing that we are not only more than conquerors but that the devil, their master, is under our feet spiritually if we know our mandate.

And he said unto them, Go ye into all the world, and preach the gospel to every creature. He that believeth and is baptized shall be saved; but he that believeth not shall be damned. And these signs shall follow them that believe; In my name shall they cast out devils; they shall speak with new tongues; They shall take up serpents; and if they drink any deadly thing, it shall not hurt them; they shall lay hands on the sick, and they shall recover. (Mark 16:15–18)

I cease not to give thanks for you, making mention of you in my prayers; That the God of our Lord Jesus Christ, the Father of glory, may give unto you the spirit of wisdom and revelation in the knowledge of him: The eyes of your understanding being enlightened; that ye may know what is the hope of his calling, and what the riches of the glory of his inheritance in the saints, And what is the exceeding greatness of his power to us-ward who believe, according to the working of his mighty power, Which he wrought in Christ, when he raised him from the dead, and set him at his own right hand in the heavenly places, Far above all principality, and power, and might, and dominion, and every name that is named, not only in this world, but also in that which is to come: And hath put all things under his feet, and gave him to be the head over all things to the church, Which is his body, the fulness of him that filleth all in all. (Eph. 1:16–23)

But God, who is rich in mercy, for his great love wherewith he loved us, Even when we were dead in sins, hath quickened us together with Christ, (by grace ye are saved;) And hath raised us up together, and made us sit together in heavenly places in Christ Jesus. (Eph. 2:4–6)

When a man puts his hands on a plough and looks back, such man is not fit for God's kingdom. He will be replaced because God's work must continue. His plans cannot be frustrated by any man, and He would rather change the man than His plans.

9. *Love for wordly possessions and positions*

We also have another set of people who refused and are still refusing to obey the call of God upon their lives because of their fat salaries or positions in the business world or politics. They think it is demeaning for them to preach the Gospel even when their peers are dying and going to hell daily. If God chooses, He may force them to obey like He did to Jonah who found himself in the belly of a fish that eventually vomited him at Nineveh's beach.

> Now the word of the LORD came unto Jonah the son of Amittai, saying, Arise, go to Nineveh, that great city, and cry against it; for their wickedness is come up before me. But Jonah rose up to flee unto Tarshish from the presence of the LORD, and went down to Joppa; and he found a ship going to Tarshish: so he paid the fare thereof, and went down into it, to go with them unto Tarshish from the presence of the LORD. But the LORD sent out a great wind into the sea, and there was a mighty tempest in the sea, so that the ship was like to be broken. (Jonah 1:1–4)

> Then Jonah prayed unto the LORD his God out of the fish's belly, And said, I cried by reason of mine affliction unto the LORD, and he heard me; out of the belly of hell cried I, and thou heardest my voice. And the LORD spake unto the fish, and it vomited out Jonah upon the dry land. (Jon. 2:1–2, 10)

Nobody told him to start preaching repentance to them. On the other hand, God may simply appoint another person to carry on His mission while heaven declares you "persona non grata." You have a choice to make before it becomes too late.

My Struggle with the Call

I remember when I had some struggles with obeying God's call for further involvement in kingdom work between 1990 and 1992 when I was already very comfortable as the audit manager of the biggest chain of newspapers (Concord Press of Nigeria) in Nigeria. I went to seminary for bachelor of theology, thinking it could satisfy God. When I finished in 1996, God fired up the pressure such that anytime I picked up any official file to deal with, I would lose my peace and hear God clearly tell me, "You are wasting your time here" over and over. My peace only returned when I picked up the Bible or any Christian book to read even in the office. When I could not bear it any longer, I finally resigned in 1996 from the job to enable me to have more time for the Gospel, and I have never regretted the decision.

Many refuse to yield in time till they have spent the best part of their lives serving people in offices, either in the political or corporate world. They may then offer themselves to God when they have retired and become spent with little or no energy left in them. God may not be too keen on investing much in such people, even assuming He has not chosen another person to carry on your assignment while you vacillated earlier. The choice is yours to make yourself available as soon as you are called and become relevant to God's program or fade into oblivion as far as God's reckoning is concerned.

CHAPTER 2

Bible Characters Substituted by God

Having written all the above about God having better substitutes to replace us if we prove unfaithful or unreliable in His calling upon us, we will carefully analyze some Bible characters that were replaced by God either because they proved unfaithful or unreliable, loved the world, abandoned ministry for fear of deaths or yielded to the flesh or Satan's temptation along the line. This will drive home the message more powerfully for those who are truly committed to the work of God, the importance of watching out for the snares and pitfalls or Satan.

1. *Elijah replaced by Elisha*

Elijah was one of the greatest prophets used mightily in many unusual ways. He was the only prophet that called fire down from heaven literally,

> Hear me, O LORD, hear me, that this people may Know that thou art the LORD God, and that thou hast turned their heart back again. Then the fire of the LORD fell, and consumed the burnt sacrifice, and the wood, and the stones, and the dust, and licked up the water that was in the trench. And when all the people saw it, they fell on their faces: and they said, The LORD, he is the God; the LORD, he is the God. (1 Kings 18:37–39)

stopped rain for three and half years, and later prayed rain down again at the appointed time.

> So Ahab went up to eat and to drink. And Elijah went up to the top of Carmel; and he cast himself down upon the earth, and put his face between his knees, And said to his servant, Go up now, look toward the sea. And he went up, and looked, and said, There is nothing. And he said, Go again seven times; And it came to pass at the seventh

time, that he said, Behold, there ariseth a little cloud out of the sea, like a man's hand. And he said, Go up, say unto Ahab, Prepare thy chariot, and get thee down, that the rain stop thee not. And it came to pass in the meanwhile, that the heaven was black with clouds and wind, and there was a great rain. And Ahab rode, and went to Jezreel. (1 Kings 18:42–45)

He was the second person in the Bible to be literally transported to heaven without experiencing physical death,

And it came to pass, as they still went on, and talked, that, behold, there appeared a chariot of fire, and horses of fire, and parted them both asunder; and Elijah went up by a whirlwind into heaven. (2 Kings 2:11)

the first being Enoch,

And Enoch walked with God: and he was not; for God took him. (Gen. 5:24)

and the third person being our blessed Lord and Savior, Jesus Christ:

And when he had spoken these things, while they beheld, he was taken up; and a cloud received him out of their sight. And while they looked stedfastly toward heaven as he went up, behold, two men stood by them in white apparel; Which also said, Ye men of Galilee, why stand ye gazing up into heaven? this same Jesus, which is taken up from you into heaven, shall so come in like manner as ye have seen him go into heaven. (Acts 1:9–11)

Yet when we closely examine the events that led God to order Elijah's replacement, we cannot but be humbled by God's way of dealing with His ministers.

Elijah had just finished calling fire down from heaven to lick up the water and sacrifice on the altar he had built (after many years of neglect) before Ahab and about four hundred and fifty false prophets of Ahab. He seized and killed them all.

> Now therefore send, and gather to me all Israel unto mount Carmel, and the prophets of Baal four hundred and fifty, and the prophets of the groves four hundred, which eat at Jezebel's table. So Ahab sent unto all the children of Israel, and gathered the prophets together unto mount Carmel. And Elijah came unto air the people, and said, How long halt ye between two opinions? if the LORD be God, follow him: but if Baal, then follow him. And the people answered him not a word. Then said Elijah unto the people, I, even I only, remain a prophet of the LORD; but Baal's prophets are four hundred and fifty men. Then the fire of the LORD fell, and consumed the burnt sacrifice, and the wood, and the stones, and the dust, and licked up the water that was in the trench. And when all the people saw it, they fell on their faces: and they said, The LORD, he is the God; the LORD, he is the God. And Elijah said unto them, Take the prophets of Baal; let not one of them escape. And they took them: and Elijah brought them down to the brook Kishon, and slew them there. (1 Kings 18:19–22, 38–40)

He thereafter went to pray for rain to fall for the first time in three and a half years. When Ahab told Jezebel (who probably did not go to the mount with them out of disdain for Elijah and his God) all that Elijah and his God did and how her false prophets fed from the king's table were killed, she was furious and promised to kill Elijah within twenty-four hours.

> And Ahab told Jezebel all that Elijah had done, and withal how he had slain all the prophets with the sword. Then Jezebel sent a messenger unto Elijah, saying, So let the gods do to me, and more also, if I make not thy life as the life of one of them by tomorrow about this time. (1 Kings 19:1–2)

Elijah ran

One would have expected the great Elijah to confront this wicked woman, having regard for the miracles he had just performed that day; but instead, he panicked, ran for his life like a common coward, abandoned his servant at Beersheba while running further by a day's journey, only sitting down probably when he became tired and exhausted.

> And when he saw that, he arose, and went for his life, and came to Beersheba, which belongeth to Judah, and left his servant there. But he himself went a day's journey into the wilderness, and came and sat down under a juniper tree: and he requested for himself that he might die; and said, It is enough; now, O LORD, take away my life; for I am not better than my fathers. (1 Kings 19:3–4)

The implications of his actions above are (i) Fear overwhelmed him and he ran, abandoning his ministry; and (ii) He also abandoned all the people who were learning under him in the school of prophets, terminating their course abruptly before graduation. Can you imagine what passed through these students' minds? They would have been despondent (to say the least) because Elijah did not even tell them where he was going, probably so that he could not be betrayed by them into the hands of Ahab and Jezebel.

Elijah grumbled and prayed an insincere prayer

In verse 4, the great Elijah grumbled bitterly, saying he has had enough and that God should take his life now. He also claimed he was not better than his fathers. We should ask which of his forefathers was a prophet of God who was enabled to call fire down or stop and start rain at his command and anoint kings. Yet he claimed not to be better than his fathers. When the flesh comes to the fore, men always exaggerate their problems and underrate the grace of God they have enjoyed.

Did Elijah really want to die? My answer is no; otherwise, why was he running away? He should have waited for Jezebel to kill him. He was not sincere in that particular prayer; it was an emotional outburst of a man overwhelmed by fear, nothing more.

> But he himself went a day's journey into the wilderness, and came and sat down under a juniper tree: and he requested for himself that he might die; and said, It is enough; now, O Lord, take away my life; for I am not better than my fathers. (1 Kings 19:4)

If God were to answer Elijah's prayer for death, imagine him missing the glorious and unique translation to heaven in a chariot of fire. What a great loss that would have been. Thank God who chooses which prayers to accede to.

One lesson i have learned from Elijah's turnaround is a confirmation of what my systematic theology lecturer taught me that "The best of men are still at best, men," meaning, no matter how spiritual a man is, he is still at his very best a man subject to the foibles of life and the flesh, which is why no man is qualified to be looked upon as a perfect example except our Lord and Savior, Jesus Christ, the author and finisher of our faith (Heb. 12:3).

God fed fleeing Elijah

Despite the fact that God was disappointed at Elijah's fear-filled flight and grumbling, he still sent an angel to feed him twice, one of which was specially prepared to sustain him for forty days and nights

> And as he lay and slept under a juniper tree, behold, then an angel touched him, and said unto him, Arise and eat. And he looked, and, behold, there was a cake baken on the coals, and a cruse of water at his head. And he did eat and drink, and laid him down again. And the angel of the LORD came again the second time, and touched him, and said, Arise and eat; because the journey is too great for thee. And he arose, and did eat and drink, and went in the strength of that meat forty days and forty nights unto Horeb the mount of God. (1 Kings 19:5–8)

without commenting, chastising, or doing anything about his prayer for death. If God were to answer or respond to many of our foolish prayer requests in moments of crisis, many of us would have finished badly, but thank God for His mercies.

Now God queries Elijah

After forty days of unfruitful flights from ministry, God finally issued His prophet a query: "What are you doing there, Elijah" (1 Kings 19:8–9)? The implication of the query is that God did not expect Elijah to be hiding there. He expected him to stand firm and confront the powers of Jezebel as he did with the false prophets.

What was Elijah's answer?

> You see God, I have been jealously fervent and passionate for your work [which he had temporarily abandoned] but the children of Israel have

killed all your prophets, I and only I am the one remaining and they wanted to kill me so I had to run. (1 Kings 19:10)

Again, let us examine the implications of his answer:

i.   It is true Elijah was passionate about God's work.
ii. It is true many prophets had been killed.
iii. Elijah considered only himself as remaining; meaning, he did not consider any of the people in his school of prophets (including the one that followed him through thick and thin till he abandoned him to his fate in Beersheba) good enough to be a prophet yet.

How many of us in ministry always think that without us, God cannot work and never consider any of our strong lieutenants of many years standing good enough to take over from us? This may be so even when it is apparent that someone needs to step in to continue the vision while we stay in the background to give wise counsel. Remember that Elijah could not have been the only one slaughtering all the four hundred and fifty false prophets at Mount Carmel; his trainee prophets were there to help. He had now abandoned all of them to an uncertain future, dashing their hopes!

God gave Elijah a second query

Apparently not satisfied with Elijah's answer to His first query, God demonstrated His power through strong winds that tore mountains into shreds, earthquakes, and fire; but God was not there yet (they were just God's outriders which many people see today and become mesmerized even when God is not involved). These demonstrations of power were probably to reassure Elijah that He is still the same all-powerful God.

By the time God spoke in a "still small voice," it was to give Elijah a second query: "What doeth thou here, Elijah" (1 Kings 19:11–13)? Elijah gave the same excuses which again did not satisfy God in verse fourteen (1 Kings 19:14).

God responded and replaced Elijah

Having failed to satisfy God as to why he had to abandon ministry with his grumblings and requests for death, Elijah left God with no other choice than to look for a replacement for him.

> And the LORD said unto him, Go, return on thy way to the wilderness of Damascus: and when thou comest, anoint Hazael to be king over Syria: And Jehu the son of Nimshi shalt thou anoint to be king over Israel: and Elisha the son of Shaphat of Abelmeholah shalt thou anoint to be prophet in thy room. And it shall come to pass, that him that escapeth the sword of Hazael shall Jehu slay: and him that escapeth from the sword of Jehu shall Elisha slay. (1 Kings 19:15–17)

From the above, God ordered him to anoint Hazael king over Syria, Jehu over Israel, and Elisha "to be prophet in thy room" so that the three of them, Hazael as political leader, Jehu, a war general, and Elisha as a spiritual leader could combine their different skills to defeat the enemies of God's plan for Israel. If God could replace Elijah, be careful; He can replace you and me.

Now the bombshell

In verse 18, God told Elijah what he had never known even as a leading prophet: that God had seven thousand prophets yet in Israel who had neither bowed their knees to Baal nor kissed him (1 Kings 19:18). What a humbling revelation it must have been for Elijah who had hitherto thought he was the only prophet remaining! In fact, Obadiah, the governor of the king's chamber, had kept one hundred prophets in caves, feeding them with probably the king's food.

> And Ahab called Obadiah, which was the governor of his house. (Now Obadiah feared the

LORD greatly: For it was so, when Jezebel cut off the prophets of the LORD, that Obadiah took an hundred prophets, and hid them by fifty in a cave, and fed them with bread and water.) (1 Kings 18:3–4)

We indeed know in part now how wonderful will it be when we shall know all in eternity. We shall indeed appreciate the reasons some things happened and that God cares more for us than we appreciate. Hallelujah.

Seven thousand hiding prophets?

Some have suggested that if the seven thousand prophets had been active publicly in speech and action, Elijah would have had some support and may not have run away in the first instance. This may be true, just as many great Christian leaders sometimes choose to keep quiet in moments of crisis when they should stand to be counted on the side of God and righteousness publicly. All that evil needs in order to thrive is for men and women who know how to do good and resist evil to keep quiet and do nothing. That these prophets' integrity is unassailable is clear from the fact that God said they had not bowed down to Baal or kissed him, but why were they quiet and unknown in the midst of such evil ravaging the land?

We can only guess that maybe their time of manifestation and ministry was not yet ripe (since God said He reserved them for Himself), or they were simply too intimidated by the powers that Jezebel and her satanic priests exercised over the kingdom through King Ahab.

Elijah chose his substitute

Elijah obeyed God and chose Elisha, who until then was tending his father's oxen, to replace him as God had commanded him.

So he departed thence, and found Elisha the son of Shaphat, who was plowing with twelve yoke

of oxen before him, and he with the twelfth: and
Elijah passed by him, and cast his mantle upon
him. And he left the oxen, and ran after Elijah,
and said, Let me, I pray thee, kiss my father and
my mother, and then I will follow thee. And he
said unto him, Go back again: for what have I
done to thee? And he returned back from him,
and took a yoke of oxen, and slew them, and
boiled their flesh with the instruments of the
oxen, and gave unto the people, and they did eat.
Then he arose, and went after Elijah, and minis-
tered unto him. (1 Kings 19:19–21)

Now, it takes greatness and humility to know it is time to choose
a successor to us in ministry without grumbling. How many ministers of God would not secretly victimize or frustrate their successors
if God shows them who their successors are to be? Many run their
ministry as if they will never leave the stage, and when they are forced
to leave either by reason of age or physical disability, they place their
surrogates or family members in the organization or church as if it
were a personal business empire. When we manipulate potential successors out for selfish reasons, God moves away and leaves us with
the empty shell of what had been a great ministry. May God help us
to manage transition with godly fear in Jesus's name (Amen). Thank
God for Elijah; he obeyed God faithfully, and the work continued
even more strongly after him.

Elijah returned to ministry

The great Elijah returned to ministry briefly apparently to train
and hand over to Elisha properly as we see in

Then Moab rebelled against Israel after the death
of Ahab. And Ahaziah fell down through a lat-
tice in his upper chamber that was in Samaria,
and was sick: and he sent messengers, and said

unto them, Go, enquire of Baalzebub the god of Ekron whether I shall recover of this disease. But the angel of the LORD said to Elijah the Tishbite, Arise, go up to meet the messengers of the king of Samaria, and say unto them, Is it not because there is not a God in Israel, that ye go to enquire of Baalzebub the god of Ekron? Now therefore thus saith the LORD, Thou shalt not come down from that bed on which thou art gone up, but shalt surely die. And Elijah departed. And when the messengers turned back unto him, he said unto them, Why are ye now turned back? And they said unto him, There came a man up to meet us, and said unto us, Go, turn again unto the king that sent you, and say unto him, Thus saith the LORD, Is it not because there is not a God in Israel, that thou sendest to enquire of Baalzebub the god of Ekron? therefore thou shalt not come down from that bed on which thou art gone up, but shalt surely die. And he said unto them, What manner of man was he which came up to meet you, and told you these words? And they answered him, He was an hairy man, and girt with a girdle of leather about his loins. And he said, It is Elijah the Tishbite. Then the king sent unto him a captain of fifty with his fifty. And he went up to him: and, behold, he sat on the top of an hill. And he spake unto him, Thou man of God, the king hath said, Come down. And Elijah answered and said to the captain of fifty, If I be a man of God, then let fire come down from heaven, and consume thee and thy fifty. And there came down fire from heaven, and consumed him and his fifty. Again also he sent unto him another captain of fifty with his fifty. And he answered and said unto him, O man of God, thus hath the king said, Come down quickly. And Elijah answered and said unto them, If I be a man of God, let fire come down from heaven, and consume thee and thy fifty. And the fire of God came down from heaven, and consumed him and his fifty. And he sent again a captain of the third fifty with his fifty. And the third captain of fifty went up, and came and fell on his knees before Elijah, and besought him, and said unto him, O man of God, I pray thee, let my life, and the life of these fifty thy servants, be precious in thy sight. Behold, there came fire down from heaven, and burnt up the two captains of the former fifties with their fifties: therefore, let my life now be precious in thy sight. And the angel of the Lord said unto Elijah, Go down with him: be not afraid of him. And he arose, and went down with him unto the king. And he said unto him, Thus saith the Lord, Forasmuch as thou hast sent messengers to enquire of Baalzebub the god of Ekron, is it not because there is no God in Israel to enquire of his word? therefore thou shalt not come down off that bed on which thou art gone up, but shall surely die. So he died according to the word of the Lord which Elijah had spoken. And Jehoram reigned in his stead in the second year of Jehoram the son of Jehoshaphat king of Judah; because he had no son.

Now the acts of Ahaziah which he did, are they not written in the book of the chronicles of the kings of Israel? (2 Kings 1:1–18)

where he called fire down to destroy the King Ahaziah's soldiers twice.

The restored Elijah goes home gloriously

It is one thing to make mistakes and another thing to make amends with men and God before the books and chapters of our lives are closed on earth. Elijah succeeded in this when one considers that God granted him a wonderful chariot of fire and horses from heaven to convey His great prophet home physically without experiencing death like all mortals.

And it came to pass, when the LORD would take up Elijah into heaven by a whirlwind, that Elijah went with Elisha from Gilgal. And Elijah said unto Elisha, Tarry here, I pray thee; for the LORD hath sent me to Bethel. And Elisha said unto him, As the LORD liveth, and as thy soul liveth, I will not leave thee. So they went down to Bethel. And the sons of the prophets that were at Bethel came forth to Elisha, and said unto him, Knowest thou that the LORD will take away thy master from thy head to day? And he said, Yea, I know it; hold ye your peace. And Elijah said unto him, Elisha, tarry here, I pray thee; for the LORD hath sent me to Jericho. And he said, As the LORD liveth, and as thy soul liveth, I will not leave thee. So they came to Jericho. And the sons of the prophets that were at Jericho came to Elisha, and said unto him, Knowest thou that the LORD will take away thy master from thy head to day? And he answered, Yea, I know it; hold ye your peace. And Elijah said unto him, Tarry, I pray thee, here; for the LORD hath sent me to Jordan. And he said, As the LORD liveth, and as thy soul liveth, I will not leave thee. And they two went on. And fifty men of the sons of the prophets went, and stood to view afar off: and they two stood by Jordan. And Elijah took his mantle, and wrapped it together, and smote the waters, and they were divided hither and thither, so that they two went over on dry ground. And it came to pass, when they were gone over, that Elijah said unto Elisha, Ask what I shall do for thee, before I be taken away from thee. And Elisha said, I pray thee, let a double portion of thy spirit be upon me. And he said, Thou hast asked a hard thing: nevertheless, if thou see me when I am taken from thee, it shall be so unto thee; but if not, it shall not be so. And it came to pass, as they still went on, and talked, that, behold, there appeared a chariot of fire, and horses of fire, and parted them both asunder; and Elijah went up by a whirlwind into heaven. (2 Kings 2:1–11)

Elijah started well and finished well as God's prophet despite his frailties. He chose a successor who continued where he left off and did double of Elijah's level of ministry.

May God help us to end the race well on earth and inherit God's kingdom hereafter in Jesus's name (Amen).

CHAPTER 3

Moses, God's Friend Replaced by Joshua

Moses was one of the greatest prophets God ever gave to humanity, so close to God that He proclaimed Moses as His friend with whom he spoke "face to face as a man speaks with his friend" (Num. 12:5–8). God did extraordinary miracles through Moses such that even after his death, God allowed the disciples to view him together with Elijah and our Lord Jesus Christ on the Mount of Transfiguration, with God Himself speaking at the scene to confirm the authenticity of the Sonship of our Lord Jesus Christ,

> And after six days Jesus taketh Peter, James, and John his brother, and bringeth them up into an high mountain apart, And was transfigured before them: and his face did shine as the sun, and his raiment was white as the light. And, behold, there appeared unto them Moses and Elias talking with him. Then answered Peter, and said unto Jesus, Lord, it is good for us to be here: if thou wilt, let us make here three tabernacles; one for thee, and one for Moses, and one for Elias. While he yet spake, behold, a bright cloud overshadowed them: and behold a voice out of the cloud, which said, This is my beloved Son, in whom I am well pleased; hear ye him. (Matt. 17:1–5)

yet God found it imperative to replace him with Joshua.

Moses' Background, Calling, and Exploits

A look into Moses's background, calling, and the great exploits he did for and with God will humble us and diminish our proud achievements into nothing.

Moses biography

1. Moses was born into a family with both parents coming from the priestly Levite family.

    And there went a man of the house of Levi, and took to wife a daughter of Levi. And the woman conceived, and bare a son: and when she saw him that he was a goodly child, she hid him three months. And when she could not longer hide him, she took for him an ark of bulrushes, and daubed it with slime and with pitch, and put the child therein; and she laid it in the flags by the river's brink. (Exod. 2:1–3)

2. Hidden and saved from death by God using pharaoh's daughter in a carefully God-ordained plot (Exod. 2:4–8).

3. Trained and raised in an Egyptian palace with his mother being paid for nursing her own son (Exod. 2:9–10). He received the best education and care available, with the Egyptian throne within his reach (Heb. 11:23–30).

4. His calling was extraordinary (Exod. 3:1–6, 10–14).

5. Moses was a one-man army that tormented pharaoh and all the powers of Egypt (the greatest military and occultic power at that time) with ten unusual plagues that climaxed with the death of the first born of all Egyptian families including even animals, finally forcing a stubborn pharaoh subdued by God's greater power to release Israel unconditionally (Exod. 12:29–33).

6. When pharaoh pursued them into the wilderness (Exod. 14:5–9), God divided the Red Sea to pave the way for Israel to *escape* while destroying pharaoh and his elite army, horses, and chariots (Exod. 14:21–28).

7. Moses turned bitter water to good, drinkable water at Marah (Exod. 5:22–25).

8. The mere raising of Moses's hands was used by God to defeat Israel's enemies at war (Exod. 17:8–13).

9. God came out forcefully and openly to rebuke and Judge Moses's senior sister, Mariam, who took it upon herself to abuse the humility and simplicity of Moses by leading a rebellion against him. God warned her Moses was His special friend with whom He spoke face-to-face as a man speaks with his friend. In fact, it took Moses's fervent pleading with God to restore her and heal the leprosy that came from God upon her instantly as punishment for such effrontery (Num. 12).

10. The ground also opened up and swallowed Dathan, Abiram, and others who challenged Moses's authority in the wilderness (Num. 16:23–35).

11. Through Moses's intercession, God made food (*manna*) fall from heaven for Israel in the wilderness (Exod. 16:11–15).

12. Moses wrote the first five books of the Bible, which include the only detailed account of how God created the world even before he was born. Till today, no other account (historical or religious) is as comprehensive and convincing as his account of creation.

13. Moses fasted forty days and forty nights twice and remained in God's presence to obtain the Law from God. His face became so luminous that Israelites were afraid to move near him till he used a veil to cover it (Exod. 34:27–32).

Moses was great yet humble and was not too ambitious, nor was he in ministry for a personal gain as are many ministers of God in our day. In fact, at a time when God became angry with Israelites' behavior in the wilderness, God decided to kill all of them, save Moses and his family, from whom God promised to make a great nation instead of Israel. Moses refused the offer of personal greatness but prayed and pleaded till God changed His mind and forgave Israel (Num. 14:11–20).

He also told God he would not go further if God did not go with them. In fact, he said God should not even take them to the promised land flowing with milk and honey if God would not go with them (Exod. 33:2–3, 15–15). This is very much unlike many of today's ministers who are busy making names for themselves and their families and would have told God, "No problem. So long as you take us to the promised land."

The promise of the presence of an angel among them was no substitute for God's presence as far as Moses was concerned. How many people have claimed to have been instructed by "angels" throughout history and have come up with heresies and clearly non-biblical teaching and practices?

What went wrong?

It is normal to wonder what the great Moses could have done wrong that could warrant his being stopped by God from entering the promised land and his replacement by Joshua.

Moses was defeated by anger

Everyone, especially God's servants must prayerfully deal with any weakness we may have before it gets us into serious trouble with God. That we are being used by God is no license for us to continue to avoid being honest about our known weaknesses. We must do all that is within our power to overcome them with God's help before we make a shipwreck of our lives and ministries.

Moses was a man who occasionally got angry when under serious provocation like you and I, but the Bible clearly warns us that even when we are angry, we must not sin: "Be ye angry, and sin not: let not the sun go down upon your wrath: Neither give place to the devil" (Eph. 4:26–27).

First angry encounter

The first time Moses got angry, he committed murder by killing the Egyptian who was mistreating an Israelite. He had to run away from the palace to Midian for fear of being dealt with by Pharaoh.

> And it came to pass in those days, when Moses was grown, that he went out unto his brethren, and looked on their burdens: and he spied an Egyptian smiting an Hebrew, one of his brethren. And he looked this way and that way, and when he saw that there was no man, he slew the Egyptian, and hid him in the sand. And when he went out the second day, behold, two men of the Hebrews strove together: and he said to him that did the wrong, Wherefore smitest thou thy fellow? And he said, Who made thee a prince and a judge over us? intendest thou to kill me, as thou killedst the Egyptian? And Moses feared, and said, Surely this thing is known. Now when Pharaoh heard this thing, he sought to slay Moses. But Moses fled from the face of Pharaoh, and dwelt in the land of Midian: and he sat down by a well. (Exod. 2:11–15)

Even if the Egyptian was wrong in beating the Israelite, should Moses have gone to the extent of killing him? The answer is a definite no. Even though God hates murder, He apparently did not punish Moses for this.

Second angry encounter

The second time Moses got seriously angry was when he came down from the mountain with God's laws on the two tablets of stone written with the finger of God.

> And the Lord repented of the evil which he thought to do unto his people.

And Moses turned, and went down from the mount, and the two tables of the testimony were in his hand: the tables were written on both their sides; on the one side and on the other were they written.

And the tables were the work of God, and the writing was the writing of God, graven upon the tables. (Exod. 32:14–16)

He had been in God's presence for forty days and forty nights without food and water, he came down only to be confronted by the fact that his people had made a golden calf and were worshipping it with outrageous revelry.

And when the people saw that Moses delayed to come down out of the mount, the people gathered themselves together unto Aaron, and said unto him, Up, make us gods, which shall go before us; for as for this Moses, the man that brought us up out of the land of Egypt, we wot not what is become of him. And Aaron said unto them, Break off the golden earrings, which are in the ears of your wives, of your sons, and of your daughters, and bring them unto me. And all the people brake off the golden earrings which were in their ears, and brought them unto Aaron. And he received them at their hand, and fashioned it with a graving tool, after he had made it a molten calf: and they said, These be thy gods, Israel, which brought thee up out of the land of Egypt. And when Aaron saw it, he built an altar before it; and Aaron made proclamation, and said, Tomorrow is a feast to the LORD. And they rose up early on the morrow, and offered burnt offerings, and brought peace offerings; and the people sat down to eat and to drink, and rose up to play. (Exod. 32:1–6)

In anger, God told Moses He would destroy Israel and make Moses a greater nation (Exod. 3:7–10). Moses rejected God's tempting offer, prayed, and begged God on behalf of Israel till God forgave them.

> And the Lord said unto Moses, Go, get thee down; for thy people, which thou broughtest out of the land of Egypt, have corrupted themselves: They have turned aside quickly out of the way which I commanded them: they have made them a molten calf, and have worshipped it, and have sacrificed thereunto, and said, These be thy gods, O Israel, which have thy fierce wrath, and brought thee up out of the land of Egypt. And the Lord said unto Moses, I have seen this people, and, behold, it is a stiffnecked people: Now therefore let me alone, that my wrath may wax hot against them, and that I may consume them: and I will make of thee a great nation. (Exod. 3:7–10)

> And Moses besought the LORD his God, and said, LORD, why doth thy wrath wax hot against thy people, which thou hast brought forth out of the land of Egypt with great power, and with a mighty hand? Wherefore should the Egyptians speak, and say. For mischief did he bring them out, to slay them in the mountains, and to consume them from the face of the earth? Turn from thy fierce wrath, and repent of this evil against thy people. Remember Abraham, Isaac, and Israel, thy servants, to whom thou swarest by thine own self, and saidst unto them, I will multiply your seed as the stars of heaven, and all this land that I have spoken of will I give unto your seed, and they shall inherit it forever. And the

LORD repented of the evil which he thought to
do unto his people. (Exod. 32:11–14)

When Moses saw the golden calf and open adultery and revelry
going on among the Israelites, God's people, called to holiness, his
anger erupted, and he broke the two tablets of stone containing the
laws he brought from God after forty days of fasting (Exod. 32:19).
He burnt the golden calf, ground it to powder, mixed it with water,
and forced the Israelites to drink it (Exod. 32:20). He also commanded the sons of Levi who sided with him to kill about three
thousand men (probably with an equal number of women) who par-
ticipated in the orgy and revelry.

> Then Moses stood in the gate of the camp, and
> said, Who is on the LORD's side? Let him come
> unto me. And all the sons of Levi gathered
> themselves together unto him. And he said unto
> them, Thus Levi gathered themselves and he
> said unto them, Thus together unto him. Arid
> he said unto them, Thus saith the LORD God of
> Israel, Put every man his sword by his side, and
> go in and out from gate to gate throughout the
> camp, and slay every man his brother, and every
> man his companion, and every man his neigh-
> bour. And the children of Levi did according
> to the word of Moses: and there fell of the peo-
> ple that day about three thousand men. (Exod.
> 32:26–28)

Moses ordered them to repent and consecrate themselves to
God while he went to plead with God for them to the point of
demanding that his name be blotted out of God's book if He did not
forgive them.

> And Moses returned unto the LORD, and said,
> Oh, this people have sinned a great sin, and have

made them gods of gold. Yet now, if thou wilt forgive their sin; and if not, blot me, I pray thee, out of thy book which thou hast written. And the LORD said unto Moses, Whosoever hath sinned against me, him will I blot out of my book. (Exod. 32:31–33)

God promised them angelic guidance but postponed their punishment till a later date.

Therefore now go, lead the people unto the place of which I have spoken unto thee: behold, mine Angel shall go before thee: nevertheless in the day when I visit I will visit their sin upon them. And the LORD plagued the people, because they made the calf, which Aaron made. (Exod. 32:34–35)

A critical review of the above scenarios leads to the following conclusions:

1. Moses had every reason to be angry; in fact, his anger emanated from what we can legitimately call righteous indignation.
2. God's anger was going to get red hot against Israel if Moses had not stepped in to intercede for Israel (Exod. 32:9–10).
3. Moses pled to the point that he was ready to sacrifice his place in God's book of life. This was the height of sacrificial ministry and love for one's people or congregation.
4. Moses got some reprieve for Israel albeit temporarily.
5. Moses who begged God not to allow His anger to wax hot was not able to control his own anger when he saw the abominations being committed.
6. His anger waxed so hot that he broke the precious stone tablets upon which the Almighty God Himself had written the law with His own finger (Exod. 32:19). Again, this action did not in any way contribute to the solution of the

problems on hand. Every other reaction of his may have been permitted by God, but breaking the stone most likely displeased God. No wonder that God made Moses cast the tables with his (Moses) own hands when he went up for a duplicate copy. He fasted another forty days and forty nights in God's presence, laboriously crafting the stone tablets before God wrote on.

> And the LORD said unto Moses, Hew thee two tables of stone like unto the first: and I will write upon these tables the words that were in the first tables, which thou brakest. And be ready in the morning, and come up in the morning unto mount Sinai, and present thyself there to me in the top of the mount. And no man shall come up with thee, neither let any man be seen throughout all the mount; neither let the flocks nor herds feed before that mount. And he hewed two tables of stone like unto the first; and Moses rose up early in the morning, and went up unto mount Sinai, as the LORD had commanded him, and took in his hand the two tables of stone. (Exod. 34:1–4)

God even reminded him that it was he who broke the first one: "which thou breakest."

We must never misuse any of our gifts and authority in ministry to seek revenge or in our anger exceed the limit of what God would consider acceptable to Him. May God help us to be temperate at all times in Jesus's name (Amen).

Third angry encounter

The third time Moses became really angry was when he was provoked in the desert of Zin when there was no water. The Israelites rebelled against Moses and Aaron, saying that Moses should have left them in Egypt where they had access to the delicacies of Egypt instead of coming to die in the wilderness without water.

> Then came the children of Israel, even the whole congregation, into the desert of Zin in the first month: and the people abode in Kadesh; and Miriam died there, and was buried there. And there was no water for the congregation: and they gathered themselves together against Moses and against Aaron. And the people chode with Moses, and spake, saying, Would God that we had died when our brethren died before the LORD! And why have ye brought up the congregation of the LORD into this wilderness, that we and our cattle should die there? And wherefore have ye made us to come up out of Egypt, to bring us in unto this evil place? it is no place of seed, or of figs, or of vines, or of pomegranates; neither is there any water to drink. (Num. 20:2–5)

Moses and Aaron, without any recorded response to these provocations, went to God who ordered him to speak to the rock before him, promising that water would come out for them (Num. 20:6–8).

Moses, out of anger, gathered the people and said, "Hear now ye REBELS, shall WE fetch you water out of this rock?" Then he probably forgot God's instructions that he should only speak to the rock (not even to the people), because he was very angry. He used the old method God gave him on an earlier occasion by striking the rock with his rod twice (Num. 20:11).

Water still gushed out for them, but God was seriously angry with Moses on this occasion and He said so, telling him that he would not get to the promised land because he did not believe Him and did not sanctify Him before the people (Num. 20:12).

The other offense that God probably could not ignore was that Moses, by his statement "must we" was literally claiming the ability to bring the water out of the rock by himself.

The Bible says the people made matter very difficult for Moses at the waters of strife because they provoked his spirit and he spoke "unadvisedly with his lips" (Ps. 106:32–33).

Lessons

This is a big lesson to us: that you were provoked is not a good excuse before God to cross the borderline into sin. God does not always use the same method all the time; we must obey all God's instructions for every situation. Moses had earlier struck a rock to bring water on God's instructions.

> And all the congregation of the children of Israel journeyed from the wilderness of Sin, after their journeys, according to the commandment of the Lord, and pitched in Rephidim: and there was no water for the people to drink. Wherefore the people did chide with Moses, and said, Give us water that we may drink. And Moses said unto them, Why chide ye with me? wherefore do ye tempt the Lord? And the people thirsted there for water; and the people murmured against Moses, and said, Wherefore is this that thou hast brought us up out of Egypt, to kill us and our children and our cattle with thirst? And Moses cried unto the Lord, saying, What shall I do unto this people? they be almost ready to stone me. And the Lord said unto Moses, Go on before the people, and take with thee of the elders of Israel; and thy rod, wherewith thou smotest the river, take in thine hand, and go. Behold, I will stand before thee there upon the rock in Horeb; and thou shalt smite the rock, and there shall come water out of it, that the people may drink. And Moses did so in the sight of the elders of Israel. (Exod. 17:1–6)

This time, the rock he struck was a theophany of Jesus Christ according to Apostle Paul (1 Cor. 10:4). Moses would normally not dare disobey God or strike Jesus Christ on His head, but under provocation, he struck Him not once but twice, and he paid dearly for it later.

Moses's sins recalled and punished, replaced with Joshua

As many of us will be tempted to believe today, we are still in good standing with God simply because God is still doing miracles and showing us great revelations today even though we harbor unconfessed and unforgiven sin. Moses continued to be used greatly by God till the end.

When it was time for God to punish Moses for the sin he has committed most likely some years before, He recalled Moses's sins and told him to get ready to die as he would not enter the promised land (Deut. 1:37–38). Moses recalled painfully that "God was angry with me for your sake."

He begged God to let him go over to the "good land, the godly mountain," yet God said no. In fact, God told him he would only see it with his eyes and forbade him to speak any more to Him on the matter, but that Joshua will lead Israel there (Deut. 3:23–28).

Moses lamented that God also swore "that I must die in this land" (i.e. the wilderness) (Deut. 4:21–22).

Moses said God told him that the day of his death was approaching, and that he should hand over to Joshua and present him to the congregation before Him (Deut. 31:14–15).

Moses was commanded to go up to Mount Abarim and Nebo and die "because ye trespassed against me. Ye shall see it but shall not go thither."

God showed Moses the land, but when he died, God buried Moses in a secret grave without anyone knowing his sepulcher, probably to prevent people from turning the place into a shrine or an idol to be worshipped because of his greatness in life.

> And the LORD said unto him, This is the land
> which I sware unto Abraham, unto Isaac, and
> unto Jacob, saying, I will give it unto thy seed:
> I have caused thee to see it with thine eyes, but
> thou shalt not go over thither. So Moses the ser-
> vant of the LORD died there in the land of Moab,
> according to the word of the LORD. And he bur-
> ied him in a valley in the land of Moab, over
> against Bethpeor: but no man knoweth of his
> sepulchre unto this day. (Deut. 34:4–6)

Moses spent his first forty years in an Egyptian palace (Acts 7:23), his next forty years in Median tending his father-in-law's sheep (Acts 7:30), and his last forty years in the wilderness, suffering all in order to get into the promised land; yet he just missed it due to anger (Deut. 34:1–7).

Moses, in his three addresses to Israel (that make up the book of Deuteronomy), spoke painfully about his regrets in missing the promised land at least six times as enumerated above. That should tell us he was not happy at the turn of events but still obeyed God in the matter of a smooth handing over. He did not start looking for his children or relations to hand over to, neither did He persecute Joshua as so many modern-day General Overseers would do if they know a potential candidate whom God seems to be positioning to take over from them. Moses had developed people whose spiritual growth did not depend on him but on God; hence, it was a smooth transition with no problem for those coming behind as some men might be tempted to do.

Moses still had time to compose God's commandments and put them into a song which he sang even in the face of death (Deut. 31:30, 32:1). How many of us could sing in such circumstances? There arose no prophet like Moses among all Israel and whom God knew face-to-face and through whom God did the great and mighty works, terrorizing the great Pharaoh and Egyptian powers (Deut. 34:10–12).

Lesson

We must never allow ourselves to be used by the devil to provoke leaders to err. Neither should any leader allow himself to be so provoked as to run foul of God's will and instructions. If God could punish his friend Moses and refuse to pardon him despite pleading, it should serve as a sober warning to all servants of God that God is no respecter of persons. Never take God's relationship for granted.

Was God too harsh on Moses? Maybe, maybe not; who are we to judge God? He alone is sovereign, and no man is qualified to question Him.

Did Moses miss heaven? I think not because several times after the death of Moses, God and our Lord Jesus Christ still spoke glowingly about Moses's person and ministry. Moreover, Jesus spoke with Moses and Elijah during the transfiguration on the Mount with Peter, James, and John present as witnesses and God the Father speaking from heaven:

> And after six days Jesus taketh Peter, James, and John his brother, and bringeth them up into an high mountain apart, And was transfigured before them: and his face did shine as the sun, and his raiment was white as the light. And, behold, there appeared unto them Moses and Elias talking with him. Then answered Peter, and said unto Jesus, Lord, it is good for us to be here: if thou wilt, let us make here three tabernacles; one for thee, and one for Moses, and one for Elias. While he yet spake, behold, a bright cloud overshadowed them: and behold a voice out of the cloud, which said, This is my beloved Son, in whom I am well pleased; hear ye him. (Matt. 17:1–5)

Can I be as lucky as Moses? I have serious doubts that anyone can be as lucky as Moses to still make heaven if we sin against God willfully. We have Moses and many examples to learn from in the Bible, the privilege of which Moses did not have. It is too risky to toy with sin, whether sinful anger or any other for that matter.

CHAPTER 4

Eli and His Sons Replaced by Samuel

Eli was a high priest specifically favored by God to occupy the positions of high priest (1 Sam. 1:9) and judge at the same time. He also had his two sons, Hophni and Phinehas, consecrated as priests during lifetime (1 Sam. 1:3). He judged Israel for forty uninterrupted years (1 Sam. 4:18).

Eli was so anointed by God that even a simple pronouncement on Hannah in prayer was used to cause the woman who had been barren to conceive and deliver a baby, Samuel, within one year.

> And it came to pass, as she continued praying before the LORD, that Eli marked her mouth. Now Hannah, she spake in her heart; only her lips moved, but her voice was not heard: therefore Eli thought she had been drunken. And Eli said unto her, How long wilt thou be drunken? put away thy wine from thee. And Hannah answered and said, No, my lord, I am a woman of a sorrowful spirit: I have drunk neither wine nor strong drink, but have poured out my soul before the LORD. Count not thine handmaid for a daughter of Belial: for out of the abundance of my complaint and grief have I spoken hitherto. Then Eli answered and said, Go in peace: and the God of Israel grant thee thy petition that thou hast asked of him. And she said, Let thine handmaid find grace in thy sight. So the woman went her way, and did eat, and her countenance was no more sad And they rose up in the morning early, and worshipped before the LORD, and returned, and came to their house to Ramah: and Elkanah knew Hannah his wife; and the LORD remembered her. Wherefore it came to pass, when the time was come about after Hannah had conceived, that she bare a son, and called his name Samuel, saying, Because I have asked him of the LORD. (1 Sam. 1:12–20)

Eli's children were vile

The sons of Eli, who, like their father, were also priests, were considered to be sons of Belial (another name for the devil), who knew not the Lord (1 Sam. 1:12). I sometimes wonder how they came to be consecrated as priest since "they knew not the Lord." They ought not to have been priests in the first instance, but perhaps they became priest due to the influence of their father. When you put a round peg in a square hole, you are bound to run into trouble. No wonder they saw the office as an opportunity to fatten themselves and conduct themselves in the most abominable way within the temple.

Their sins

1. They forcefully took raw meat even before the fat is burnt unto God (1 Sam. 2:13–17).
2. They committed adultery with the women that came to the temple door with seeming impunity (1 Sam. 2:22).

Eli's feeble warning

Eli heard all the evil things his children were doing with the women and sacrifices. He called and verbally warned them of the ominous implications of their effrontery and sins. Yet they ignored their father's warning because they seemed destined for destruction.

> And he said unto them, Why do ye such things? for I hear of your evil dealings by all this people. Nay, my sons; for it is no good report that i hear: ye make the LORD's people to transgress. If one man sin against another, the judge shall judge him: but if a man sin against the LORD, who shall intreat for him? Notwithstanding they hearkened not unto the voice of their father, because the Lord would slay them. (1 Sam. 2:23–25)

They continued, probably knowing their father would not do more than issue a verbal warning.

Eli got the yellow card

After Eli's verbal warning failed to curb the excesses of his children, God sent another man of God to warn him (1 Sam. 2:27–36). From the above verses, the following can be seen:

1. God reminded him that He chose Moses, Aaron, and all Levites who were Eli's forefathers from among the twelve tribes to be a specially consecrated unto Himself and gave them all the offering made by fire of the children of Israel (1 Sam. 2:27, 28).
2. Eli was honoring his children above God by tolerating their desecration of the sacrifices (1 Sam. 2:28).
3. God decided to cancel or terminate the covenant of exclusive/perpetual priesthood He made with Eli's ancestors. Since they despised God, He would also lightly esteem them (v. 30).
4. God promised to cut off the arms of Eli, the strength of his father's house, and said that they would all die young (v. 32).
5. Any man not cut off would be a pitiable caricature who will bring sadness to whoever sees him, and they would die just when they should be blossoming as flowers (v. 33).
6. Hophni and Phinehas should die the same day (v. 34). It is noteworthy that God did not tell Eli here that he too would die the same day.
7. God promised He would raise up a faithful priest unto himself to replace the household of Eli (v. 35).
8. His family members who used to have exclusive control of the priesthood office would prostrate themselves and beg for bread and silver and any priestly portion at all so that they might eat a piece of bread (v. 36).

The above are alarming enough to make the fear of God strike any man who really is of a contrite spirit, who trembles at God's words (Isa. 66:1–2). But with Eli's children, it was business as usual, and Eli still would not be moved to discipline them beyond a verbal rebuke within the confines of the family house.

Now the red card

The situation degenerated to the point that God was no longer talking to people as before. The word of God became so precious (scarce) that there were no more open visions (1 Sam. 3:1). Eli became physically blind (1 Sam. 3:2) to complete the deadly cycle, having been spiritually deaf and blind up to now.

God sent the young Samuel

Once God had written off Eli's family, God turned to the young Samuel in Eli's house who had not polluted himself.

> And the LORD came, and stood and called as at other times, samuel, Samuel. Then Samuel answered, Speak; for thy servant heareth.
> And the LORD said to Samuel, Behold, I will do a thing in Israel, at which both the ears of every one that heareth it shall tingle. In that day I will perform against Eli all things which I have spoken concerning his house: when I begin, I will also make an end. For I have told him that I will judge his house for ever for the iniquity which he knoweth; because his sons made themselves vile, and he restrained them not. And therefore I have sworn unto the house of Eli, that the iniquity of Eli's house shall not be purged with sacrifice nor offering forever. (1 Sam. 3:10–14)

From the above verses, the following are discernible:

1. God promised to start implementing His judgment upon the house of Eli for the iniquity which he knew about but tolerated (vv. 12–14).
2. That in spite of God's earlier warning, Eli's sons made themselves vile, and Eli did not restrain them (v. 13). The implication of this is that God did not consider the verbal warning Eli gave his children as a good enough restraint expected of a God-fearing priest in view of God's ominous warnings. Eli, as chief priest, had the power to distance himself from his children's misadventures and dismiss them from office publicly, but he chose to retain them because they were his children. How many men of God elevate their unqualified children to lofty offices today and retain them to the detriment of God's kingdom? A word is enough for the wise.
3. God swore that the iniquities of Eli's house had gone beyond that which could be purged or cleansed by any sacrifice forever (v. 14).

Eli's contemptuous response

After Eli forced Samuel to tell him everything God told him, you would expect Eli to be contrite and tremble at the sad news from God, not him. He had gone beyond the point of redemption: "And Samuel told him every whit, and hid nothing from him. And he said, It is the LORD: let him do what seemeth him good" (v. 18). He was ready for the worst from God but never reckoned with the fact that he was also going to be a victim of the judgment on his children and couldn't care if everyone's life was cut short in his prime. After all, he (Eli) was already old. What a pitiable way of reasoning!

A day of God's fury

When God turns his back on anyone, the most feeble enemy will overrun his or her camp with ease. The Philistines came against Israel in Aphek and smote Israel like an easy prey. When four thousand men were slaughtered in battle, they sent for the Ark of the Lord, thinking that would save the day, but it did not help.

> And the word of Samuel came to all Israel. Now Israel went out against the Philistines to battle, and pitched beside Ebenezer: and the Philistines pitched in Aphek. And the Philistines put themselves in array against Israel: and when they joined battle, Israel was smitten before the Philistines: and they slew of the army in the field about four thousand men. And when the people were come into the camp, the elders of Israel said, Wherefore hath the LORD smitten us today before the Philistines? Let us fetch the ark of the covenant of the LORD out of Shiloh unto us, that, when it cometh among us, it may save us out of the hand of our enemies. (1 Sam. 4:1–3)

Whenever a child or servant of God is living in disobedience, no prayer formula will work until he or she is reconciled to God. The enemy will always ride roughshod over them. The Philistines killed thirty thousand Israelites, the rest fled, and they seized the ark of God from them, killing Hophni and Phinehas.

> And the Philistines fought, and Israel was smitten, and they fled every man into his tent: and there was a very great slaughter; for there fell of Israel thirty thousand footmen. And the ark of God was taken; and the two sons of Eli, Hophni and Phinehas, were slain. (1 Sam. 4:10–11)

Now the bad news

Eli at ninety-eight years heard about the defeat of Israel and the death of his two vile sons and was apparently too stunned to react emotionally. However, when told that the ark of God had been taken by the enemy, it was too much for him, he fell backwards, broke his neck, and died.

> And the man said unto Eli, I am he that came out of the army, and I fled today out of the army. And he said, What is there done, my son? And the messenger answered and said, Israel is fled before the Philistines, and there hath been also a great slaughter among the people, and thy two sons also, Hophni and Phinehas, are dead, and the ark of God is taken. And it came to pass, when he made mention of the ark of God, that he fell from off the seat backward by the side of the gate, and his neck brake, and he died: for he was an old mam and heavy. And he had judged Israel forty years. (1 Sam. 4:16–18)

Phinehas's wife, who was pregnant, entered into a crisis induced labor when she heard about all the evils which had befallen the family in a single day. She gave birth and died after naming the child Ichabod, meaning, the glory is departed from Israel.

A sad end indeed

It was a sad end indeed for a family that had such glorious covenants cancelled, losing four key members of the family in one day and suffering the permanent loss of the priestly office. They were grievous losses, but it happened because they ignored God's warnings.

Lessons

The lessons below can be gleaned from the disaster that befell Eli's household:

1. Never put unqualified, unregenerate and untested people in positions of authority in God's kingdom work (no matter the temptation), as a result of blood relationship or friendship or even monetary gifts. It always ends up hunting those who do so (1 Tim. 5:22).
2. Do not hesitate to discipline or remove anyone who abuses his or her privileged office.
3. Eli is not recorded as committing any sin personally other than the fact that he practiced parental indulgence. He was not spared by God when His hammer fell.

God holds everyone responsible for the sins committed within their jurisdiction. An example is Abraham who was commanded of God to circumcise all males under his roof, whether they be slaves or sons.

> This is my covenant, which ye shall keep, between me and you and thy seed after thee; Every man child among you shall be circumcised. And ye shall circumcise the flesh of your foreskin; and it shall be a token of the covenant betwixt me and you. And he that is eight days old shall be circumcised among you, every man child in your generations, he that is born in the house, or bought with money of any stranger, which is not of thy seed. He that is born in thy house, and he that is bought with thy money, must needs be circumcised: and my covenant shall be in your flesh for an everlasting covenant. And the uncircumcised man child whose flesh of his foreskin is not circumcised, that soul shall be cut off from

his people; he hath broken my covenant. (Gen. 17:10–14)

Abraham compelled everyone to circumcise even in adulthood with him showing the way at over ninety-nine years of age.

Those who go to church leaving their children at home for the devil to use as his workshop don't know what risks they are taking at all. Anyone who is not ready to serve the living God with you does not deserve to live under your roof.

> Now therefore fear the LORD, and serve him in sincerity and in truth: and put away the gods which your fathers served on the other side of the flood, and in Egypt; and service ye the LORD. And if it seem evil unto you to serve the LORD, choose you this day whom ye will serve; whether the gods which your fathers served that were on the other side of the flood, or the gods of the Amorites, in whose land ye dwell: but as for me and my house, we will serve the LORD. And the people answered and said, God forbid that we should forsake the LORD, to serve other gods. (Josh. 24:14–16)

4. Whenever God starts sending warning messages to His child or servant through a third party instead of talking to you directly, it is time to tremble at God's word, repent, and run back to God without any further delay. That was the undoing of Eli's household.
5. On no account must we dare God like Eli did for it is indeed a fearful thing to fall into the hands of the living God (Heb. 10:31).
6. Relying on so called Christian tokens, Philacteries, special oil, anointed cloths, etc. will fail us if we live in disobedience to God. The ark of God that killed Uzzah when he touched it (not being a priest) was taken by Philistines

from Israel without any immediate death. If God is not with you, putting on the Urim and Thumnim won't help you hear God. Take a lesson from King Saul.

7. God found a replacement for Eli's family in the person of the young Samuel who was not yet born when Eli and his children had started ministering in the offices of high priest and priests respectively. God has a substitute for everyone in His vineyard who disobeys, you and I included. May God help us to discharge our kingdom responsibilities with the fear of God and receive our reward at the end of our earthly service from God, in Jesus's name (Amen).

CHAPTER 5

Judas Iscariot's Loss, Matthias's Gain

Judas Iscariot is one name nobody on earth wants to bear. You may see people bearing Judas (which actually is the Greek form of Judah which means "praised," a name borne by six people in the Holy Bible) but not Judas Iscariot.

How did his name and personality become so loathsome today? A critical look into the Bible will show us why. Please join me as we take a sobering excursion into the Bible's account of the life and death of this man who could have had an important role in the history of Christianity, not only in this world but also in eternity.

Great privileges that came his way

Judas Iscariot had the following uncommon privileges which he squandered like those who never value what they have until they lose it.

1. Judas was a chosen and empowered apostle of the Lord Jesus Christ. One of the first twelve that were taught and empowered directly by our Lord Jesus Christ. He was commissioned to preach the Gospel, heal the sick, and cast out demons (Matt. 10:1–8; Luke 9:1–10).
2. He obtained a part of the ministry of our Lord Jesus Christ (Acts 1:17) as a preacher and healer (Mark 6:7–13; Luke 9:10).
3. He was the first treasurer of the disciples and our Lord Jesus Christ Himself—a very privileged position of trust which he abused by stealing even from the all-knowing Jesus Christ (John 12:4–6, 13:29).
4. He witnessed firsthand all the outstanding miracles of our Lord Jesus, including walking on water, raising the dead, commanding the storm, and healing lepers, lame, and the blind.

How did Judas become a willing tool in the hand of Satan?

Given all the above privileges, one cannot but ask: What happened along the way that made him commit the greatest mistakes of all time?

1. *He became a thief.* Judas Iscariot's privilege of being the treasurer of the Lord Jesus Christ and His disciples exposed his weakness. Covetousness led him to start stealing from the funds entrusted to his care (John 12:3–6). He only protested Mary's pouring costly ointment on Jesus as a waste because he wanted the opportunity to steal the proceeds.

2. *Jesus's rebuke probably offended him.* If you look at the following verses, you will see that Jesus Christ, knowing his ulterior motives, gave Judas Iscariot an open rebuke which probably did not go down well with him (John 12:3–6; Mark 14:3–9). In the next verse, disappointed and smarting under the rebuke, he left to cut a deal with his master's enemies (Mark 14:10–11).

3. *Satan entered into Judas.* Satan entered into Judas Iscariot, prompting him to see an opportunity to make money for himself (Luke 22:3–6). All he was required to do was to inform the plotters when Jesus Christ would be free from the multitudes so that his arrest would not be resisted by the crowd or lead to street riots. Jesus Christ's enemies could not believe their luck, they grabbed the rare opportunity with both hands and promised him thirty pieces of silver (Mark 14:12–6).

4. *Rejected a timely warning.* Jesus Christ warned Judas Iscariot of the consequences of his betrayal, but he was too greedy, setting his eyes on what thirty pieces of silver could buy, to consider the eternal implications of his actions (Mark 14:18–21).

5. *Exposed, he stormed out.* When he discovered that his secret deal was not hidden from his master after all, he stormed out to execute the deal instead of repenting (John 13:30).

How many people storm out of the church because they did evil and rejected a timely warning and discipline?

6. *Betrayed his master with a kiss.* Jesus's enemies dared not arrest him publicly because of the attendant public protest that would follow. Not prepared to take any risks, Judas told them about a personal retreat by Jesus Christ and His disciples to Gethsemane. The place provided the best opportunity for a smooth arrest without any uproar (Matt. 26:47–50). Did you notice that he kissed Jesus Christ, a supposed show of affection, yet Jesus Christ still called him "friend" in verse 50? What a compassionate Jesus who would not be offended by such monumental betrayal.

7. *He felt guilty.* Some have suggested maybe Judas thought Jesus would disappear and not be apprehended in view of his enormous power, hence, he would still have the money having done his part. We cannot be sure of this. What we know from the scriptures is that Judas felt guilty, probably tried to undo it by returning the money, but it was too late (Matt. 27:1–4). He returned the money but could no longer return to the disciples. Even his paymasters snubbed him when he complained that he had betrayed innocent blood (Matt. 27:4–7).

8. *Satan-possessed Judas hanged himself.* Having failed to undo the havoc he had committed and under a burden of guilt, he did not repent; instead, the devil that had entered into him pushed him further to hang himself (Matt. 27:3–5).

9. *Hanged at the plot bought with his blood money.* The chief priests and elders refused to accept the blood money. Judas was forced to cast it down on the floor of the temple and left to hang himself. He could not even live to spend the money on whatever project the devil deceived him he could use the money for. The priests then used the money to buy a plot of land to bury strangers (Matt. 27:5–8). Peter told us that Judas used the money to buy a plot of land. Is there any contradiction here? No. Since the money rightly belonged to Judas Iscariot, the implication is that the chief

priests buying the land did not change anything; it still belonged to Judas Iscariot. It is therefore no coincidence that Judas hanged himself in the plot of land and burst asunder in the midst, with his bowels gushing out (Acts 1:18).

Satan, in his characteristic way of mocking his servants after he considers them expendable (having finished using them), must have led him to that very plot of land (Luke 22:3). If you serve the devil, he will eventually destroy you. That is part of his three point agenda: to kill, steal, and destroy (John 10:10).

Judas ruined himself

Judas Iscariot, by his actions, ruined himself and wasted so many opportunities and divine privileges, some of which are as follows:

1. He saw Jesus's arrest but did not witness the wonderful resurrection and defeat of death and the grave by Jesus Christ (Matt. 28:1–7).
2. He missed an opportunity to witness the glorious ascension of the risen Lord (Acts 1:9).
3. He missed the house prepared for him in heaven (John 14:1–4).
4. He has been regretting and suffering in hell for over two thousand years till now, with no end in sight for his pitiable predicament as it is going to be his everlasting experience.

Lessons from Judas's fall

Judas lost because he refused to be saved through his own avarice and stubborn refusal to come to Christ even after his crime. Even though he regretted his action, saying, "I have sinned, I betrayed an innocent blood" (Matt. 27:3–4), many go this far in regret, but they never obtain forgiveness because they do not go to God through Christ's blood and renounce sin. True repentance goes beyond being

88

sorrowful for sin. It entails confessing the sins, turning away from them, and turning to God through Christ for the forgiveness of those sins.

Judas allowed his desires to place him in a position where Satan could manipulate him. Do not agree to serve in any position that will expose you to temptation in any area you are yet to overcome in your life or with which you are still struggling. A man with problems of financial integrity should not accept a treasureship position lest Satan take advantage of his exposure to destroy him.

Judas became a pretender at some point in his ministry. Initially, Judas obtained part of the ministry from Jesus (Acts 1:17) but lost out when the devil was able to manipulate his carnal desires and ambitions (John 17:12).

Why did Judas betray Jesus Christ? Destiny?

There have been many debates through the ages as to why Judas betrayed Jesus Christ. Different theories and suggestions have been made by Bible scholars, the most prominent based on the fact that Judas's betrayal had been prophesied before he was born and even before the incarnation of the Lord Jesus Himself. The following scriptures attest to the fact: "Yea, mine own familiar friend, in whom I trusted, which did eat of my bread, hath lifted up his heel against me" (Ps. 41:9). The question to be answered is why should it be Judas Iscariot who would fulfill this ignominious role? Why not any of the other disciples or even a total stranger to the group?

The truth is that even if an item is destined to be stolen, it will take a thief to fulfill such a prophecy. Someone who has all the qualities and a tendency that Satan can easily capitalize upon to fulfill such a role. If the strong-room door of a bank is left open to the public, it is a big temptation for people passing by to steal, but it is only the spiritually weak who will be tempted to loot it. Others will still pass by and refuse to touch it because they know something more than what money can buy is at stake, even our relationship with our Savior in heaven. After all, what shall it profit a man, if he gains the whole world but loses his soul?

My humble submissions

While not claiming to be a Bible scholar, the following is my own humble contribution as to the possible reasons why Judas betrayed his master.

Confusion about Jesus's mission

Many people were confused as to the real mission and character of our Lord Jesus Christ when He started ministry. Some thought he was going to be a political leader who would liberate them from the grip of the Roman colonial rulers or oppressive kings of His day, setting them free, maybe employing military units or fighters. This was so even though He explicitly stated His mission.

> The Spirit of the Lord is upon me, because he hath anointed me to preach the gospel to the poor; he hath sent me to heal the brokenhearted, to preach deliverance to the captives, and recovering of sight to the blind, to set at liberty them that are bruised, To preach the acceptable year of the Lord. And he closed the book, and he gave it again to the minister, and sat down. And the eyes of all them that were in the synagogue were fastened on him. And he began to say unto them, This day is this scripture fulfilled in your ears. And all bare him witness, and wondered at the gracious words which proceeded out of his mouth. And they said, Is not this Joseph's son? And he said unto them, Ye will surely say unto me this proverb, Physician, heal thyself: whatsoever we have heard done in Capernaum, do also here in thy country. And he said, Verily I say unto you, No prophet is accepted in his own country. (Luke 4:18–24)

They still believed that he would eventually get to the point of confronting political institutions on their behalf.

Some examples will suffice:

1. *John the Baptist.* Even though John the Baptist, His cousin in the flesh, knew, accepted, and proclaimed Jesus's messianic mission (Matt. 3:11–15; John 3:26–30), heard God speak directly from heaven, and saw Holy Spirit like a dove descending on Jesus from heaven (Matt. 3:16–17), he apparently became confused when Herod put him (John the Baptist) in prison, and Jesus did not confront him. He sent some of his disciples to Jesus to ask Him if He was the Messiah, or they should start looking for another one instead (Matt. 11:2–3). Jesus sent a reply (Matt. 11:4–6). After this, John the Baptist did not send for any further proof.

2. *Herod.* Herod killed many innocent children in a futile attempt to kill the baby Jesus, thinking he had come take his throne away from him (Matt. 2:1–3; Matt. 2:16–18).

3. *They wanted to make him king*: Some of those who benefited from His bread and miracles attempted to install Him as King, but He refused and escaped (John 6:12–15).

4. *His disciples.* Even Jesus's disciples, those closest to Him, had to ask Him at one point, "Look, we have left everything and followed you, what shall be our gain?" (Matt. 19:27–29). Jesus's answer in verses 28 and 29, promising them thrones and everlasting life, was probably not fully understood by all or always did not fully fit the expectation of Judas Iscariot. I said this because even after the death and resurrection of our Lord and Savior, Jesus Christ, when He was addressing the disciples (Acts 1:4–8), they still asked Him whether He would now restore again the kingdom to Israel (v. 6). It showed they were still seeing political leadership as part of His ministry with them as potential, if not full government ministers, with attractive portfolios.

Jesus quickly redirected their attention to their real need—power for service (vv. 7–8).

Before this, they had left ministry disillusioned and returned back to fishing, which they had left at Jesus's command some years before at the time of their calling. This move was led by Peter, the most prominent among them (John 21:1–7). If Peter and the others had known the real reason Jesus came, they would have known that He had fulfilled his mission and left the rest for them to continue. Take a close look at Cleopas's disillusionment even after Jesus's resurrection (Luke 24:13–14).

Judas's possible expectations

Judas Iscariot may have expected huge financial and political returns from his association with Jesus's ministry and probably projected many mansions he intended building for himself; hence, he had been stealing from the purse steadily (John 12:4–6). Then suddenly, Jesus started talking about His death, which might signify the end to His access to free money from the purse. Disillusioned, he must have thought: "Where does that leave me?" A bitter spirit which turned to hate when he saw his ambitions being thwarted, must have pushed him to try to save himself. Who knows the mind of man? The heart of man is indeed most deceitful and desperately wicked (Jer. 17:9–11). No wonder he left riches without even spending them, he lost everything, and his hopes ended in tragedy.

What are your expectations?

People enter into or join ministries for various reasons and motives. Some may even be in sharp contrast to those of the leaders of those ministries. When those expectations are not met over the time set by themselves, some leaders abandon the path of truth and righteousness, deviating from the objects of ministry for selfish reasons. Some even go into occult practices to attract crowd, money and fame, contrary to scripture, and some abandon ministry completely. Jesus said no one that lays his hands on the plough and looks back is fit for the kingdom (Luke 9:62). This sober statement must be considered by all those who enter the ministry with less than noble motives. Some disillusioned followers, on the other hand, may become disruptive to the progress of the kingdom work if their leader will not veer from the noble path of truth and righteousness. Instead of becoming a Judas betraying their leaders or promoting discord and ending on the same platform with Judas Iscariot, it is better to repent or leave quietly so that God's judgment will not fall on them.

Did Jesus know Judas's role?

It is normal to ask whether Jesus Christ knew the dubious roles Judas was playing behind his back. How he was stealing and eventually would betray Him. If He knew, why did He not remove Judas from being the treasurer or stop him from betraying Him? These are legitimate questions which we shall consider in view of what is revealed in the scriptures.

Jesus was and is omniscient

Jesus Christ, as the second Person of the Trinity, was and is still omniscient. He even knew what people thought in their hearts (Matt. 9:4; Luke 9:47–48). He confirmed that Judas was the devil's agent (John 6:70–71). Jesus positively identified Judas as the betrayer and warned him of the consequences (Matt. 26:20–25; John 13:21–27). Though Jesus warned him, He allowed Judas to make up his mind so that the scriptures might be fulfilled (Isa. 53:1–7).

God-in-like manner has the power to compel all human beings to worship Him alone, but He having made us free moral agents will not violate His rule; He gave everyone opportunities to hear the Gospel and then decide what they want to do with the sacrifice of Jesus. Even though God would not want anyone to perish but that all would come to the knowledge of truth, He will not force anyone either (1 Tim. 2:3–6). Everyone of us must face the consequences of our actions when He comes soon (Rev. 22:11–14).

His bishopric let another take

God does not always change His plans which He has set from eternity. What God has always done is to replace any individual who fails Him or becomes obstructive or irrelevant to the progress of His kingdom.

Finally, the apostles gathered to prayerfully find a replacement for Judas Iscariot.

> And in those days Peter stood up in the midst of the disciples, and said, (the number of names together were about an hundred and twenty,) Men and brethren, this scripture must needs have been fulfilled, which the Holy Ghost by the mouth of David spake before concerning Judas, which was guide to them that took Jesus. For he was numbered with us, and had obtained part of this ministry. Now this man purchased a field with the reward of iniquity; and falling headlong, he burst asunder in the midst, and all his bowels gushed out. And it was known unto all the dwellers at Jerusalem; insomuch as that field is called in their proper tongue, Aceldama, that is to say, The field of blood. For it is written in the book of Psalms, Let his habitation be desolate, and let no man dwell therein: and his bishoprick let another take. Wherefore of these men which have companied with us all the time that the Lord Jesus went in and out among us, Beginning from the baptism of John, unto that same day that he was taken up from us, must one be ordained to be a witness with us of his resurrection. And they appointed two, Joseph called Barsabas, who was surnamed Justus, and Matthias. And they prayed, and said, Thou, Lord, which knowest the hearts of all men, shew whether of these two thou hast

chosen, That he may take part of this ministry and apostleship, from which Judas by transgression fell, that he might go to his own place. And they gave forth their lots; and the lot fell upon Matthias; and he was numbered with the eleven apostles. (Acts 1:15–26)

Peter lamented how Judas, a man who had obtained a share in the ministry from Jesus Christ and was numbered among the first twelve (vv. 16–17), lost out to greed and died a shameful death (vv. 18–20). Someone had to be chosen to take his bishopric (v. 20), so the church, according to the scriptures, prayed, voted, and ordained Mathias to replace Judas Iscariot as an apostle.

Those who voted were one hundred and twenty which included the remaining eleven apostles, Mary the mother of Jesus, and His brethren who joined Jesus' ministry later (Acts 1:14-15).

A gradual fall

Did you notice that Judas Iscariot did not just wake up one day to take his own life? His fall from grace to the pit of hell was a gradual one, from being a chosen apostle, preacher, healer, and exorcist to a disillusioned thief and hypocrite then a betrayer, conspiring in the murder of his master and finally a self-destructive suicide.

Watch out and retrace your steps back to Jesus Christ the moment you notice your first spiritual decline or when someone draws your attention to it. Selfish self-defense can only lead to a greater slide into spiritual decay.

What a painful loss. It should make us become sober minded about all we do in the kingdom, knowing that God can summon a replacement for everyone who disappoints Him, including even you and me.

CHAPTER 6

Saul Fell, David Took Over

A privilege misused

Israel never had a king until they insisted on one, and God gave them Saul, the son of Kish, who was the tallest and most handsome man in Israel, head and shoulders above every other man. (1 Sam. 9:2). Saul was simply looking for his father's lost ass when he was told of the choice and anointed king (1 Sam. 10:1, 5–6, 9–10). He was not expecting it at all, and even those who saw him prophesying could not help asking, once Saul became a prophet, "Is Saul also among the prophets?" (1 Sam. 10:11–12).

It was indeed a privilege for Saul to occupy such an exalted position without asking for it. In fact, Saul considered himself and his tribe to be the least in Israel, quite undeserving of the lofty proposals of the prophet Samuel.

> And Samuel answered Saul, and said, I am the seer: go up before me unto the high place; for ye shall eat with me to day, and tomorrow I will let thee go, and will tell thee all that is in thine heart. And as for thine asses that were lost three days ago, set not thy mind on them; for they are found. And on whom is all the desire of Israel? Is it not on thee, and on all thy father's house? And Saul answered and said, Am not I a Benjamite, of the smallest of the tribes of Israel? and my family the least of all the families of the tribe of Benjamin? wherefore then speakest thou so to me? (1 Sam. 9:19–22)

Saul impulsively offered sacrifice

After two years on the throne, the Philistines gathered thirty thousand chariots and six thousand horsemen and other innumerable footmen against Israel (1 Sam. 13:5). Overwhelmed by the sheer numerical strength and the weapons of their enemies, the men of Israel started deserting the war zone (1 Sam. 13:6–7).

Saul waited for seven days then sent for the prophet Samuel to make a peace offering for them before the war broke out. Seeing that more men were deserting him, he impulsively but wrongly assumed the role of the priest and offered a burnt offering to God (1 Sam. 13:8–9). As soon as he had finished, Samuel came and questioned him. Saul claimed he was "forced" to offer the burnt offering because Samuel delayed, and the people were deserting him in droves (1 Sam. 13:10–12).

Saul ventured into another ministry for which he was not ordained by God. How many of us are struggling to operate in ministries we are not called into by God just because we fear we may not gather or retain the crowd we think we require to make an impact in life and ministry? Are you sure God called you into the type of ministry you are operating, or you are there because it is fashionable or financially more rewarding than your original calling? Reflect soberly and retrace your steps.

Saul fell from grace to grass

Samuel told Saul he had acted foolishly, and that God would have established his kingdom upon Israel forever (1 Sam. 13:13). With Saul's impulsive disobedience, his kingdom came to an abrupt end because God had chosen another man who was after His own heart to replace him (1 Sam. 13:14). What a very sad way to end a promising monarchy after just two years! How many ministers struggle in other people's callings just because they are more prominent or visible instead of staying where God called them? Nobody wants to be a Father Nash anymore; people don't know when to stop in their quest for wealth and prominence. It is sad indeed, to say the least.

Saul fails God in the next assignment

You would have expected Saul to have learned his lesson and never to disobey God, but he had not. In the next assignment, God told him to go with the soldiers and kill all living souls, including animals in Amalek, and that he should not spare anything (1 Sam.

15:1–3). Saul spared Agag, the Amalekites' king, the best of the sheep, oxen, fat hogs, lambs, and all that were good, destroying all things and killing people he considered not good (1 Sam. 15:7–9).

Saul denies responsibility

God became angry at Saul's apparent disregard for His instructions, regretting making Saul king (1 Sam. 15:10-11). Having been confronted by the prophet Samuel, Saul not only lied that he indeed had carried out God's instructions, but also lied that all the animals and things Samuel saw with him were spared and taken as spoils of war by the people to sacrifice unto God.

> And Saul said unto Samuel, Yea, I have obeyed the voice of the LORD, and have gone the way which the LORD sent me, and have brought Agag the king of Amalek, and have utterly destroyed the Amalekites. But the people took of the spoil, sheep and oxen, the chief of the things which should have been utterly destroyed, to sacrifice unto the LORD thy God in Gilgal. (1 Sam. 15:20–21)

Saul had the effrontery to argue with the prophet Samuel in verse 20 above, practically exonerating himself.

God's hammer falls again

God rebuked Saul through the prophet Samuel, telling him that obeying Him is more valuable than foolish sacrifice (1 Sam. 15:22), and that God had also rejected him from being king (1 Sam. 15:23). When Samuel made to leave, Saul grabbed his garment which was torn in his hand. This made the prophet Samuel pronounce on him that his government had been taken from him and given to a neighbor who is better than him (1 Sam. 15:27–28).

False repentance

Saul claimed to be penitent, but his immediate request showed he was not. He wanted Samuel to window-dress him and his fallen government by following him to worship the Lord publicly, to give a semblance of normalcy before the people (1 Sam. 15:30–31). Did you notice how he said "yet honour me now" and "follow me to worship 'thy God'" in verse 30 above? He was still thinking of himself alone, even the God who appointed him became "thy God." His public image became more important to him than the grim judgment that had just been spoken by God's mouthpiece against him and his government.

Samuel maintained dignified distance

Not only did Samuel refuse to follow Saul to offer a sacrifice that was just meant to be a public relations stunt; he stopped visiting Saul in the palace from that day till Saul died. He maintained a dignified distance (1 Sam. 15:35). This is a lesson that some servants of God need to learn from the prophet Samuel. Many hobnob with the rich and powerful people and political leaders all over the world for temporary gain despite their sinful lifestyles. They can't summon the courage to tell them the truth and the mind of God. You see, God's servants craving the attention and patronage of political leaders in high places sometimes condemn them publicly but encouraging them in their evil privately. In those days, when a Samuel, an Elijah, or an Elisha showed up in the city, the king trembled to meet them, asking whether all was well. Until such assurance was given, the king's mind would not be at peace. Now we write and lobby them regularly just to get a highly patronizing response and maybe a pittance. Lord, have mercy.

David anointed king while Saul sat on the throne

God ordered the prophet Samuel to anoint David as king while Saul was yet alive, sitting on the throne (1 Sam. 16:1, 16:12–13). The Spirit of God came upon David from that day forward.

Evil spirit torments King Saul

While Saul still acted as king, sitting on the throne and enjoying the perquisites and courtesies attached to the office of reigning King, the Spirit of the Lord had departed from Saul. Because nature hates a vacuum, a demonic spirit took over Saul's remaining miserable life (1 Sam. 16:14–15). Did you notice in the verses above that Saul's servants immediately saw behind the façade put up by Saul? They sensed the presence of an evil spirit in him and advised that David be brought to drive away the evil spirit in him and with his anointed musical skill (1 Sam. 16:16-19, 21-23).

Whenever something goes wrong with our spiritual lives, concerned people around us will notice it. We need not pretend all is well. Let us be humble enough to admit it and receive help where necessary. Nobody is infallible, and we should not pretend to have all the solutions ourselves when it is obvious we need help from other brethren and servants of God.

David kills Goliath. Saul is jealous

David killed Goliath, the Philistine champion who had defied Saul and the army of Israel for forty days with no one finding the courage to confront his intimidating stature and boastful mouth. The women innocently sang the praises of David more than Saul's, and the spirit of jealously made Saul angry and fretful that the throne might be given to David (1 Sam. 18:6–9). Yet unknown to him, God had actually given the throne to David even before he was invited to the palace.

Saul plotted David's death

Saul made several attempts to kill David, but all failed.

> And it came to pass on the morrow, that the evil
> spirit from God came upon Saul, and he prophe-
> sied in the midst of the house: and David played

with his hand, as at other times: and there was a javelin in Saul's hand. And Saul cast the javelin; for he said, I will smite David even to the wall with it. And David avoided out of his presence twice. And Saul was afraid of David, because the LORD was with him, and was departed from Saul. Therefore Saul removed him from him, and made him his captain over a thousand; and he went out and came in before the people. And David behaved himself wisely in all his ways; and the LORD was with him. Wherefore when Saul saw that he behaved himself very wisely, he was afraid of him. But all Israel and Judah loved David, because he went out and came in before them. And Saul said to David, Behold my elder daughter Merab, her will i give thee to wife: only be thou valiant for me, and fight the LORD's battles. For Saul said, Let not mine hand be upon him, but let the hand of the Philistines be upon him. (1 Sam. 18:10–17)

After many other plots failed, Saul plotted to kill David by himself by inviting him to dinner, but David did not show up, having arranged with Jonathan, Saul's son but a bosom friend of David, to stay away (1 Sam. 20:27–29).

Saul was very angry with Jonathan, claiming that David was a threat to Jonathan's chances of ever becoming king in the future, as if it was a family throne that must be occupied by his descendants (remember Saul was never a prince before becoming a king?) (1 Sam. 20:30–31).

When Jonathan told Saul, his father, that David did not deserve death, his anger got the better of him, and he threw a javelin at him with the aim of killing his own son (1 Sam. 20:32–33).

Lesson

How many servants of God have killed or frustrated potential leaders out of the ministries run by them in a desperate attempt to ensure that their children take over the leadership from them instead of those they consider outsiders to the family? No wonder many ministries start wobbling and eventually die after their founding fathers, mothers passed to glory (i.e. died).

Saul ought to have recognized David as the part of God's program for Israel, but no, he preferred to kill him. The truth is that God arranged to bring David to the palace to do what I call industrial training, to learn and familiarize himself with palace duties and ethics, including war roles so that he would be thoroughly prepared to assume the kingship when the divinely appointed time came.

Saul spent time and resources, trailing David even in forests and on mountains with David being so magnanimous as to spare Saul's life when he had the opportunity to kill him in his sleep.

Saul seeks witchcraft help

In chapter 28 of 1 Samuel, we see Saul fretting because the Philistines, his traditional enemies, came out against him again. With David chased out of the army and palace, Samuel dead, there was no one he could turn to. In desperation, Saul went to inquire from God how to proceed with the battle, but God, who cannot be fooled, did not answer him. He tried dreams, Urim, and the prophets all to no avail.

> And when Saul saw the host of the Philistines, he was afraid, and his heart greatly trembled. And when Saul enquired of the LORD, the LORD answered him not, neither by dreams, nor by Urim, nor by prophets. (1 Sam. 2:5–6)

He then sought a witch's help. He had to disguise and go to her by night to try to conjure the spirit of Prophet Samuel who was dead to assist him.

> Then said Saul unto his servants, Seek me a woman that hath a familiar spirit, that I may go to her, and enquire of her. And his servants said to him, Behold, there is a woman that hath a familiar spirit at Endor. And Saul disguised himself, and put on other raiment, and he went, and two men with him, and they came to the woman by night: and he said, I pray thee, divine unto me by the familiar spirit, and bring me him up, whom I shall name unto thee. And the woman said unto him, Behold, thou knowest what Saul hath done, how he hath cut off those that have familiar spirits, and the wizards, out of the land: wherefore then layest thou a snare for my life, to cause me to die? And Saul sware to her by the LORD, saying, As the LORD liveth, there shall no punishment happen to thee for this thing. Then said the woman, Whom shall I bring up unto thee? And he said, Bring me up Samuel. (1 Sam. 28:7–11)

Now the final judgment

When the spirit that Saul perceived to be that of the dead Prophet Samuel came up, his verdict was highly unwelcome to Saul.

> And the king said unto her, Be not afraid: for what sawest thou? And the woman said unto Saul, I saw gods ascending out of the earth. And he said unto her, What form is he of? And she said, An old man cometh up; and he is covered with a mantle. And Saul perceived that it was Samuel, and he stooped with his face to the ground, and bowed himself.

> And Samuel said to Saul, Why hast thou disquieted me, to bring me up? And Saul answered, I am sore distressed; for the Philistines make war against me, and God is departed from me, and answereth me no more, neither by prophets, nor by dreams: therefore I have called thee, that thou, mayest make known unto me what I shall do. Then said Samuel, Wherefore then dost thou ask of me, seeing the LORD is departed from thee, and is become thine enemy? And the LORD hath done to him, as he spake by me: for the LORD hath rent the kingdom out of thine hand, and given it to thy neighbour, even to David: Because thou obeyedst not the voice of the LORD, nor executedst his fierce wrath upon Amalek, therefore hath the LORD done this thing unto thee this day. Moreover the LORD will also deliver Israel with thee into the hand of the Philistines: and tomorrow shalt thou and thy sons be with me: the LORD also shall deliver the host of Israel into the hand of the Philistines. (1 Sam. 28:13–19)

While I do not want to join the debate as to whether this was actually Samuel's spirit or not in this book, there is no doubt that the verdict totally tallies with the previous pronouncements of God on Saul. The predictions of death on him and others in battle were exactly fulfilled the following day. Saul committed suicide after he was wounded in a battle while the sons he was desperately positioning for the throne after him were also killed (1 Sam. 31:1–6). The Philistines not only cut off the head of Saul, they brought his armor into their idol's house and publicly displayed his head around the countryside while fastening his body to the wall of Beth-Shan (1 Sam. 31:8–10). It was such a sad end for King Saul that David wept and composed a classical elegy.

> And David lamented with this lamentation over Saul and over Jonathan his son: (Also he bade them

teach the children of Judah the use of the bow:
behold, it is written in the book of Jasher.) The
beauty of Israel is slain upon thy high places: how
are the mighty fallen! Tell it not in Gath, publish
it not in the streets of Askelon; lest the daughters
of the Philistines rejoice, lest the daughters of the
uncircumcised triumph. Ye mountains of Gilboa,
let there be no dew, neither let there be rain, upon
you, nor fields of offerings: for there the shield
of the mighty is vilely cast away, the shield of
Saul, as though he had not been anointed with
oil. From the blood of the slain, from the fat of
the mighty, the bow of Jonathan turned not back,
and the sword of Saul returned not empty. Saul
and Jonathan were lovely and pleasant in their
lives, and in their death they were not divided:
they were swifter than eagles, they were stronger
than lions. Ye daughters of Israel, weep over Saul,
who clothed you in scarlet, with other delights,
who put on ornaments of gold upon your
apparel. How are the mighty fallen in the midst
of the battle! O Jonathan, thou wast slain in thine
high places. I am distressed for thee, my brother
Jonathan: very pleasant hast thou been unto me:
thy love to me was wonderful, passing the love
of women. How are the mighty fallen, and the
weapons of war perished! (2 Sam. 1:17–27)

David eventually became king, waxing stronger and stronger
while the house of Saul was finished (2 Sam. 3:1, 5:1–5).

Lessons from Saul's fall

1. Saul was serially disobedient to God's instructions. There
    is a limit to how long God will tolerate any disobedient
    servant. A time will come when no sacrifice will avail.

2. Saul probably became too familiar with God and the prophet Samuel. Having watched how Samuel performed the sacrifice, he thought he could do it as well. Unknown to him, it is not the mechanical motions and the physical items presented that really matter. He burnt his fingers. Jumping into ministries you are not anointed to handle can be dangerous.

3. Carrying on ruling after God had rejected him was a big affront to God. He should have abdicated even if for some time while repentantly seeking God's forgiveness, mercy, and possible reinstatement. No wonder he was thoroughly disgraced by God. Once you know you have fallen into sin or away from God, no matter how big your position is in ministry, be humble enough to step aside, confess to God and the relevant bodies in the ministry so that they can pray and seek God's face with you. Who knows? God who said He will have mercy upon whom He will have mercy can still extend His magnanimity to you. To continue ministering can leave you exposed to fatal satanic attacks.

4. Recognize and encourage those God sends your way to help you succeed in ministry. Do not see them as threats, neither should you persecute nor chase them out of the ministry. God is the one who ultimately decides the fate and future of everyone around you. Enjoy their confidence and recognize their efforts/labor of love while it lasts. Even if you have to part ways, make it as smooth as possible to the extent it lies within your power.

5. Saul's impulsive nature tended to make him overstep his bounds. Never take important decisions impulsively, especially when under pressure, when consumed by fear or anger. Deeply reflect on the immediate and future implications of all our major decisions and actions in ministry. Remember how the gentle and humble Moses spoke unadvisedly under intense provocation, and he missed the promised land (Ps. 106:32–33).

6. Above all, obey God in all His instructions to you, no matter how painful they are to you or your personal interests. Once you know what God wants, you don't have any right to vary it. God is the owner of His work, not you.

CHAPTER 7

Balaam
Lost
to Avarice

Balaam was one of the Old Testament prophets who, though not an Israelite, was privileged to speak to and hear from God like all prophets. However, he was willing to obey God's command as long as he could profit from doing so. While acknowledging the supremacy of God Almighty, he had his heart set on the wealth he could make from Moab using his unique gift and position.

Balaam, the mercenary prophet

Balaam was a mercenary prophet who, for the love of reward, accepted King Balak's assignment to come and spiritually cripple Israel by cursing them first. Balak thought this would enable him to overcome Israel in battle. He did this because he had heard how Israel had trounced all the strong nations that confronted them on their journey to the promised land.

> And the children of Israel set forward, and pitched in the plains of Moab on this side Jordan by Jericho. And Balak the son of Zippor saw all that Israel had done to the Amorites. And Moab was sore afraid of the people, because they were many: and Moab was distressed because of the children of Israel. And Moab said unto the elders of Midian, Now shall this company lick up all that are round about us, as the ox licketh up the grass of the field. And Balak the son of Zippor was king of the Moabites at that time. He sent messengers therefore unto Balaam the son of Beor to Pethor, which is by the river of the land of the children of his people, to call him, saying, Behold, there is a people come out from Egypt: behold, they cover the face of the earth, and they abide over against me: Come now therefore, I pray thee, curse me this people; for they are too mighty for me: peradventure I shall prevail, that we may smite them, and that I may drive them

out of the land: for I wot not that he whom thou
blessest is blessed, and he whom thou cursest is
cursed. (Num. 22:1–7)

God warned Balaam not to go (Num. 22:8–13). Having been
offered a great reward, he went again to seek God's permission for
an assignment he knew God had expressly disapproved. God gave
him permission to go on one condition: he must only say what God
would tell him to say, nothing more (Num. 22:14–20).

His ass spoke with human voice

Glad to get God's permissive approval, he set out in the morning, riding his ass which stopped and turned aside from the journey,
having seen the angel of the Lord with a sword blocking the road.
God's anger was kindled against Balaam for going. God's permissive will can be dangerous. Being too blinded by the prospect of a
wrongful gain, Balaam did not see the angel and the danger ahead.
He struck the poor ass after it had crushed his foot against the wall
till it was forced to stand up to him, speaking with a human voice to
rebuke the blind prophet (Num. 22:21–30; 2 Pet. 2:15–16).

Eyes opened

God opened Balaam's eyes to see the angry angel with a sword
who rebuked him for his perverse ways and for smiting the ass three
times. Instead of fully repenting, he offered a partial apology, offering
to turn back "if it displeases thee" (v. 34) as if he did not know how
unacceptable his mission was to God. How else could God have com-
municated His disapproval? Balaam still had his eyes on the rewards
from Balak. Balaam's greed got the best of him, so that even the fact
that his obedient ass stood up to him, speaking with a human voice
did not shock or startle him enough to humble him.

Balaam ate humble pie

When Balaam got to see Israel in the camp, he opened his mouth to curse, only to have his mouth taken over by God, blessing Israel, and prophesying a great future for Israel to the consternation of Balak, his paymaster, and all the princes of Moab who were standing right beside him.

> And God met Balaam: and he said unto him, I have prepared seven altars, and I have offered upon every altar a bullock and a ram. And the LORD put a word in Balaam's mouth, and said, Return unto Balak, and thus thou shalt speak. And he returned unto him, and, lo, he stood by his burnt sacrifice, he, and all the princes of Moab. And he took up his parable, and said, Balak the king of Moab hath brought me from Aram, out of the mountains of the east, saying, Come, curse me Jacob, and come, defy Israel. How shall I curse, whom God hath not cursed? or how shall I defy whom the LORD hath not defied? For from the top of the rocks I see him, and from the hills I behold him: lo, the people shall dwell alone, and shall not be reckoned among the nations. Who can count the dust of Jacob, and the number of the fourth part of Israel? Let me die the death of the righteous, and let my last end be like his! And Balak said unto Balaam, What hast thou done unto me? I took thee to curse mine enemies, and, behold, thou hast blessed them altogether. And he answered and said, Must I not take heed to speak that which the LORD hath put in my mouth? (Num. 23:4–12)

Balak could not believe his ears as he expressed his anger and queried the mercenary prophet.

Balaam, upon hearing promises of greater rewards, made other sacrifices, on different altars, a bullock and a ram on an altar in seven different places to get God to change His mind, all to no avail. He was forced to admit his inability to curse Israel.

> And when he came to him, behold, he stood by his burnt offering, and the princes of Moab with him. And Balak said unto him, What hath the LORD spoken? And he took up his parable, and said, Rise up, Balak, and hear; hearken unto me, thou son of Zippor: God is not a man, that he should lie; neither the son of man, that he should repent: hath he said, and shall he not do it? or hath he spoken, and shall he not make it good? Behold, I have received commandment to bless: and he hath blessed; and I cannot reverse it. He hath not beheld iniquity in Jacob, neither hath he seen perverseness in Israel: the LORD his God is with him, and the shout of a king is among them. God brought them out of Egypt; he hath as it were the strength of an unicorn. Surely there is no enchantment against Jacob, neither is there any divination against Israel: according to this time it shall be said of Jacob and of Israel, What hath God wrought! Behold, the people shall rise up as a great lion, and lift up himself as a young lion: he shall not lie down until he eat of the prey, and drink the blood of the slain. And Balak said unto Balaam, Neither curse them at all, nor bless them at all. But Balaam answered and said unto Balak, Told not I thee, saying, All that the LORD speaketh, that I must do? (Num. 23:17–26)

Yet another altar

You would have thought that at this point, Balaam would stop, but his greed was so great that he still followed Balak to try another sacrifice of seven bullocks and seven rams.

He gives up his dirty pursuit

After knowing that God would remain faithful to His people no matter who was doing the devil's bidding against them, Balaam stopped seeking curses against Israel (Num. 24:1). He now continually prophesied a great future for Israel till both Balak and the mercenary prophet parted ways in disappointment.

> How goodly are thy tents, O Jacob, and thy tabernacles, O Israel! As the valleys are they spread forth, as gardens by the river's side, as the trees of lign aloes which the LORD hath planted, and as cedar trees beside the waters. He shall pour the water out of his buckets, and his seed shall be in many waters, and his king shall be higher than Agag, and his kingdom shall be exalted. God brought him forth out of Egypt; he hath as it were the strength of an unicorn: he shall eat up the nations his enemies, and shall break their bones, and pierce them through with his arrows. He couched, he lay down as a lion, and as a great lion: who shall stir him up? Blessed is he that blesseth thee, and cursed is he that curseth thee. And Balak's anger was kindled against Balaam, and he smote his hands together: and Balak said unto Balaam, I called thee to curse mine enemies, and, behold, thou hast altogether blessed them these three times. Therefore now flee thou to thy place: I thought to promote thee unto great honour; but, lo, the LORD hath kept thee back

from honour. And Balaam rose up, and went and returned to his place: and Balak also went his way. (Num. 24:5–11, 25)

Balaam revealed the secret of Israel's fall

Out of frustration and being unable to get the desired rewards, Balaam committed a grave error by accepting the wages of unrighteousness for his services, teaching Balak the secret of what would make God curse and turn His back on Israel (Jude 11). He taught him to get beautiful women to entice Israel to whoredom and to tempt Israel to worship and eat things offered to idols (Rev. 2:14). Balak and his people used these strategies until in His anger, God caused many Israelites to perish in a plague (Num. 31:16).

Balaam ended badly

Though Balaam was allowed to go back to his home safely, God waited for the appropriate time to punish him for his sins. Balaam had prayed to die the death of the righteous so that his end would be like theirs when he understood the future of Israel,

> And he took up his parable, and said, Balak the king of Moab hath brought me from Aram, out of the mountains of the east, saying, Come, curse me Jacob, and come, defy Israel. How shall I curse, whom God hath not cursed? or how shall I defy, whom the LORD hath not defied? For from the top of the rocks I see him, and from the hills I behold him: lo, the people shall dwell alone, and shall not be reckoned among the nations. (Num. 23:7–10)

but instead, Balaam later died by the sword of the Israelites in a war against the Medianites. At God's command, all the males were killed with their kings.

115

And they warred against the Midianites, as the
LORD commanded Moses; and they slew all the
males. And they slew the kings of Midian, beside
the rest of them that were slain; namely, Evi, and
Rekem, and Zur, and Hur, and Reba, five kings
of Midian: Balaam also the son of Beor they slew
with the sword. (Num. 31:7–8)

Even though we may not be able to determine Balaam's immediate successor, I am convinced that God, who would not leave His
work without a witness, was able to call on many others to continue
His work.

Lessons

1. Balaam was a man who had revelations even with his eyes
    wide open several times in the scriptures. He heard God
    clearly and prophesied with clinical precision but lost his
    life and ministry to greed, disobedience, and a mercenary
    attitude to the work of God. How many ministers of God
    are ready to pray and "prophesy" good things for those liv-
    ing unrighteously in our generation for money and posi-
    tion? Sadly, they are many. I just hope you are not one of
    them.
2. It is not good to start pestering God for a matter He has
    spoken about clearly to us already in the hope that God
    will change his mind. Balaam almost died on the way when
    God became angry at him for going even though He had
    earlier told him to go and speak only what He put in his
    mouth.
3. The stakes may be very high and tempting, but never go
    against your Maker's revealed will for temporary gain.
    Eternity is more precious than any material gain. What
    shall it profit a man who gains the whole world and loses
    his soul? said our Master Jesus.

4. As a contemporary of the great Moses and Aaron, even as a non-Israelite, Balaam had the chance to write his name in gold, but he failed and wrote it in dust. No wonder I am yet to find anyone in our day proud to adopt his name or give it to his/her children.

5. It may take some time. God is never in a hurry. He will punish sin if anyone refuses to repent. Balaam's day of recompense came, and he died, leaving everything he must have acquired through his mercenary prophetic ministry, most likely without a planned heir. The war must have caught up with him at home unprepared, as I am convinced, that Balaam was not the type of personality who would come out to face war. What a shame. What a pitiful way to end an otherwise glorious prophetic ministry in the midst of a largely ungodly community.

CHAPTER 8

Maggots Fed on King Herod

God is the one who lifts people up and brings them down at His will. He reigns in the affairs of men, and no matter what position one attains, it is with God's approval or permission.

> The LORD maketh poor, and maketh rich: he bringeth low, and lifteth up. He raiseth up the poor out of the dust, and lifteth up the beggar from the dunghill, to set them among princes, and to make them inherit the throne of glory: for the pillars of the earth are the LORD's, and he hath set the world upon them. (1 Sam. 2:7–8)

Such a person must be careful not to arrogate unto himself the glory and roles that exclusively belong to God. God will not share his glory with anyone (Isa. 4:28). No wonder God dealt decisively with King Herod. It was so swift that no one was left in doubt who rules in the affairs of men.

It happened that Herod Agrippa, because of his feeling of insecurity in the face of the rapid growth of the church, used his position to provoke the church by killing James, the brother of John. When he noticed that many Jews, especially the Rabbis, were happy, he arrested Peter and imprisoned him, waiting to execute him after Easter (Acts 12:1–4). The church rose up to pray to God who eventually sent an angel to rescue Peter miraculously (Acts 12:5–11).

Angry Herod commits blasphemy

When Herod discovered, to his chagrin, that Peter was gone, he ordered the soldiers killed (Acts 12:19). Still in an angry mood, he sought to punish Tyre and Sidon, two cities that depended on Herod for material support. In fact, he ruled over them like a colonial master. The people scurried to Blastus, the king's chamberlain, to help them appease the king. On the set day, Herod, arrayed in his royal attire, made a speech before the people who apparently were trembling before him.

Flattery

Flattery is the art of praising someone too much or in an insincere manner in order to gain favor or excessive insincere compliments.

Shrewdly, the people thought of how to praise him so that he would forgive them. They claimed his oratorical power was so great that his voice was the voice of a god and not of a man.

> And Herod was highly displeased with them of Tyre and Sidon: but they came with one accord to him, and, having made Blastus the king's chamberlain their friend, desired peace; because their country was nourished by the king's country. And upon a set day Herod, arrayed in royal apparel, sat upon his throne, and made an oration unto them. And the people gave a shout, saying, It is the voice of a god, and not of a man. (Acts 12:20–22)

Angered by Herod's acceptance of deity, God sent an angel who smote him on the spot, and maggots supernaturally and ate him before his audience. You can imagine the horror in the faces of these flatterers, but the word of God grew and multiplied (Acts 12:23–24). Needless to say, when another king took over, he knew he had to be careful with the church of God.

Lesson

In the course of ministry, no matter how highly anointed you become or how many outstanding miracles are happening when you minister, you must be careful not to take the glory that belongs to God or allow people to turn you into a deputy god, let alone accept claims of deity.

Modern Herods

There have been many modern Herods who claimed to be either Jesus Christ or God, most of whom died shamefully. The most recent was the case of a preacher in Ogba Area of Lagos, Nigeria, who claimed to be Jesus come the second time. He not only claimed he would never taste death; he claimed most of the attributes of deity. Do you know what? When his cup was full, one day, he was struck dead right in the pulpit as he blasphemed before his ignorant congregation. They took his body home and started vigils, claiming he would rise from the dead. When the putrefying odor of his dead body was becoming an embarrassment to the landlords in the area, they had to step in and force them to bury his decomposing body after about four days. God is too jealous to share His glory with anyone, so be very careful.

Learn not to flatter anyone as God hates flattering lips (Prov. 28:26). Neither should you ever be tempted to accept any claims to deity no matter how appealing it may be. It is a deceit of the devil. Even though your ego and feeling of self-importance may be pumped up, before you know it, you will become so ruined that you will be wondering how you could have so suddenly found yourself in such depths of disgrace (if you are still alive at all).

Whenever we become proud of our own abilities and achievements, not recognizing them as gifts from God, we repeat Herod's sins. Suffice to say that even his death made the word of God grow and multiply among the people (Acts 12:2–4).

CHAPTER 9

Samson Fell at the Feet of a Woman

Samson was a child of promise announced by an angel of God before his conception after his mother had been barren for many years.

> And the children of Israel did evil again in the sight of the LORD; and the LORD delivered them into the hand of the Philistines forty years. And there was a certain man of Zorah, of the family of the Danites, whose name was Manoah; and his wife was barren, and bare not. And the angel of the LORD appeared unto the woman, and said unto her, Behold now, thou art barren, and bearest not: but thou shalt conceive, and bear a son. Now therefore beware, I pray thee, and drink not wine nor strong drink, and eat not any unclean thing: For, lo, thou shalt conceive, and bear a son; and no razor shall come on his head: for the child shall be a Nazarite unto God from the womb: and he shall begin to deliver Israel out of the hand of the Philistines (Judg. 13:1–5)

God gave conditions under which he would be enabled to accomplish the task of delivering his people from the Philistines who were occupying the land given to Israel by God.

The conditions included:

1. No razor shall touch his hair (i.e. no shaving all his life).
2. His mother must not drink wine or eat any unclean thing.
3. Samson shall be a Nazarite unto God, consecrated for God's special assignments.

The Holy Spirit came upon Samson from time to time to anoint him for extraordinary feats (Judg. 13:24–25). One day, when a young lion charged at Samson, the Spirit of God filled him with power so that he killed the lion with bare hands (Judg. 14:5–6). On another occasion, he killed one thousand enemies with the ordinary jaw bone of an ass (Judg. 15:14–15).

Now Samson boasts

Like many people, Samson could not resist the temptation to become proud after such a feat.

> And Samson said, With the jawbone of an ass, heaps upon heaps, with the jaw of an ass have I slain a thousand men. And it came to pass, when he had made an end of speaking, that he cast away the jawbone out of his hand, and called that place Ramathlehi. (Judg. 15:16–17)

Pride can cause us to take credit for work we have done only through God's strength. This is one great danger every servant of God should strive to avoid.

Samson strays after a harlot

Samson, a judge in Israel, found time for such frivolities as straying into a harlot's home to sleep overnight in the camp of his enemies, neglecting his crucial duties to relax with a foreign woman.

> Then went Samson to Gaza, and saw there an harlot, and went in unto her. And it was told the Gazites, saying, Samson is come hither. And they compassed him in, and laid wait for him all night in the gate of the city, and were quiet all the night, saying, In the morning, when it is day, we shall kill him. And Samson lay till midnight, and arose at midnight, and took the doors of the gate of the city, and the two posts, and went away with them, bar and all, and put them upon his

shoulders, and carried them up to the top of an hill that is before Hebron. (Judg. 16:1–3)

Word quickly went round of the general's presence, and they locked the city gate against him while keeping vigil to watch over his movements. When Samson showed up at midnight, none of those men dared move near him. They only watched helplessly as Samson pulled out the gate, posts, bars, and all, carried it up to the hill before dropping it and going his way.

Samson marries Delilah

If Samson ever learned any lesson from the attempt by his Philistine enemies to capture him, it was not apparent, as he moved again to marry Delilah, daughter of a Philistine and the third woman he is recorded to have been involved with. He did not know that the leaders of the Philistines had planted Delilah to entice him, discover the source of his power, and neutralize him so that they would finally be able to overcome this one-man army (Judg. 16:4–5).

Samson's marriage disaster

Rejecting parental warnings and advice to choose a wife from among his people, Samson (having lost his first proposed marriage) eventually settled for Delilah, another daughter of his enemies.

Having been promised eleven hundred pieces of silver from each of the Philistine leaders, Delilah wasted no time in getting to work. She bluntly asked Samson to identify the source of his awesome power and what could be done to neutralize it.

> And it came to pass afterward, that he loved a woman in the valley of Sorek, whose name was Delilah. And the lords of the Philistines came up unto her, and said unto her, Entice him, and see wherein his great strength lieth, and by what means we may prevail against him, that we may

> bind him to afflict him: and we will give thee
> every one of us eleven hundred pieces of silver.
> And Delilah said to Samson, Tell me, I pray thee,
> wherein thy great strength lieth, and wherewith
> thou mightest be bound to afflict thee. (Judg.
> 16:4–6)

Samson thought he was too smart for such a cheap question and was sure that he could always handle her. He lied to her that if he were bound with seven green ropes that were never dried, his power would be gone (Judg. 16:7). The leaders of the Philistines, in no time, were there with ropes; in fact, they were lying in wait while Delilah was with Samson in the bedroom tying him. Delilah awoke Samson after tying him up with an alarm that the Philistines were there to kill him (Judg. 16:8–9). Samson got up, and the ropes melted as if by fire, and his adversaries fled to safety.

Angry Delilah is deceived again

It was a very furious Delilah who confronted Samson playing the victim, claiming to have been mocked by Samson's lying to her. Instead of Samson confronting her with charges of betrayal and threat to his life and ministry, he told her another lie, claiming that tying him with fresh ropes would neutralize his power.

> And Delilah said unto Samson, Behold, thou
> hast mocked me, and told me lies: now tell me,
> I pray thee, wherewith thou mightest be bound.
> And he said unto her, If they bind me fast with
> new ropes that never were occupied, then shall I
> be weak, and be as another man. Delilah there-
> fore took new ropes, and bound him therewith,
> and said unto him, The Philistines be upon thee,
> Samson. And there were liers in wait abiding in
> the chamber. And he brake them from off his
> arms like a thread. (Judg. 16:10–12)

Again, the same scenario played itself out. He escaped, only to tell another lie that fastening or wearing his seven locks, fastened with a web, would do the trick.

> And Delilah said unto Samson, Hitherto thou hast mocked me, and told me lies: tell me wherewith thou mightest be bound. And he said unto her, If thou weavest the seven locks of my head with the web. And she fastened it with the pin, and said unto him, The Philistines be upon thee, Samson. And he awaked out of his sleep, and went away with the pin of the beam, and with the web. (Judg. 16:13–14)

From the above, it should have been clear to Samson that his wife had a deadly agenda against him, but he was too confident of his ability to maintain the hide-and-seek game. For how long would he be able to do that?

The final straw

Having failed three times, Delilah became sentimental, appealing to Samson's emotions. She claimed if Samson really loved her, he would not keep the secret of his power away from her. She pestered him and nagged him daily till Samson's wall of defense collapsed, and he suddenly gave all his secrets away (Judg. 16:15–17).

Delilah then wasted no time in making Samson sleep on her lap, only to shave his hair locks off. After collecting the promised money, she called the leaders of the Philistines in to finish off their most dreaded enemy (Judg. 16:18–19).

Presumptuous Samson woke up to grim reality

Samson woke up and promised to shake himself as he used to do so that the anointing for his supernatural strength would come. The Bible says he did not know that the Lord had departed from him

(Judg. l6:20). What a grim reality that started unfolding. It all happened so rapidly that Samson must have thought it was a bad dream and that he would soon wake up. But it was neither a dream nor a stage drama but the stark reality.

Samson arrested and blinded

In no time, the great and dreadful Samson was arrested, his two eyes forcibly plucked out of their sockets, bound with brass, and compelled to grind for his new masters (yes, the Philistines). Samson would have been a great spectacle to behold. They probably could not believe who their new prisoner was. I can imagine curious Philistines paying their fare to travel from many of their cities to confirm the good news personally, hurling abuse at him, his people and his God. What a pitiable sight Samson would have made.

Samson became an entertainment dancer

The Philistine lords gathered to celebrate their unusual victory; they drank and sang praises to Dagon their god for the big catch (Judg. 16:23–24). When the celebration reached its peak, one of them remembered it would be fun to have Samson entertain them by dancing. The fallen giant was called in for a dance of shame before them and Dagon. They called the dance "sport," but to Samson and to those who believed in God, it was a painful embarrassment and a sober warning to all that from then on, the Philistines had no one to fear again. The Israelites could expect more regular military confrontations and raids on their farms.

Samson prayed

Samson's hair had started growing during the time he was imprisoned (Judg. 16:22). During the dance of shame before over three thousand men and women (probably including children),

Samson prayed to God to grant him strength again, only this once, to deal with all those responsible for his painful predicament.

> And Samson said unto the lad that held him by the hand, Suffer me that I may feel the pillars whereupon the house standeth, that I may lean upon them. Now the house was full of men and women; and all the lords of the Philistines were there; and there were upon the roof about three thousand men and women, that beheld while Samson made sport. And Samson called unto the LORD, and said, O Lord God, remember me, I pray thee, and strengthen me, I pray thee, only this once, O God, that I may be at once avenged of the Philistines for my two eyes. (Judg. 16:26–28)

Did you notice why Samson wanted vengeance in verse 28? It was for his two eyes that were plucked out. What can a totally blind general do in battle except to be taken captive or killed by even the weakest of the opposing soldiers? As I write, I can feel some of the pains that Samson felt. May God help us not to fall into the hands of our adversaries or ever be at their mercy in Jesus's name (Amen).

Samson killed them all

God, being the one who answers prayers that are in line with His purposes, wasted no time in granting him supernatural strength. At once, Samson held the pillars and pulled the house down on himself and all the lords of the Philistines; over three thousand of them, none escaped. They all died along with Samson (Judg. 16:29–30). Though the Bible says he killed more here than he had ever killed all the time he was still a strong fighter and judge over Israel, this was definitely not the end that God would have wanted for Samson.

Samson is buried

With no one to stop them, Samson's relations searched through the rubble, recovered his battered body and buried it. That was really an anticlimax for the career of a man who had judged Israel for twenty years.

Lessons

i. Never even consider breaking any part of your covenant with God. Samson broke just one promise, and that was enough to destroy him.

ii. Listen and give proper consideration to all godly counsel (whether from fellow ministers or parents) when it comes to issues of marriage. Samson definitely knew from the Law that God had forbidden Israelites from marrying from among their unbelieving idol worshiping neighbors but did not care. Passion was running at its peak, so reason had to give way. Did you notice that his three women were all Philistines? There is no record of any affair with any Israelite woman. Can you imagine how many beautiful Israelite women would have been dying to became Mrs. Samson during his success? He ignored them all. This should be a lesson for our men and women who go outside the church to marry unbelievers, thinking they will convert them later. The reverse is usually the case, so never be unequally yoked with unbelievers.

Be ye not unequally yoked together with unbelievers: for what fellowship hath righteousness with unrighteousness? and what communion hath light with darkness? And what concord hath Christ with Belial? or what part hath he that believeth with an infidel? And what agreement hath the temple of God with idols? for ye are the temple of the living God; as God hath said, i will dwell in them, and walk in them; and I will be their God, and they shall be my people. Wherefore come out from among them, and be ye separate, saith the Lord, and touch not the unclean thing; and I will receive you, And will be a Father unto you, and ye shall be my sons and daughters, saith the Lord Almighty. (2 Cor. 6:14–18)

iii. Samson was a great judge and a powerful one-man army who spent his last days grinding grain in his enemy's prison, blinded. It must have been so painful to him that he prayed that God should let him avenge "my two eyes."

iv. Samson's record is not all negative. At least he had his name etched in gold in the hall of fame in Hebrews chapter 11. He also had enough wisdom to return to God and pray. His hair started growing again.

Any time you miss God, no matter how much you have gone astray, be humble enough to acknowledge your sins, repent and return to God. He will abundantly pardon. God may also restore you fully into ministry once again as the gifts and calling of God are without repentance (Rom. 11:25).

Samson prayed to die

I believe Samson could still have been saved by God if he had not prayed to die with the Philistines. The Lord who kept Israel in Goshen while ravaging Egypt with plagues is capable of doing that.

God granted Samson his prayer, but you don't have to repeat Samson's mistakes. Unless God decides otherwise, a fallen but repentant soldier is more useful to God alive than dead.

Be wise to carefully choose your prayer points in distress! It is not over until it is over. Be guided by this song that teaches that in this race to eternity, though the flesh make you stumble and fall, rise up again and move forward. God's grace is sufficient for you.

> In the race of the prize, fainting soul
> Though a weary you bow down the knee
> Rise again and press on to the goal
> My grace is sufficient for thee
> Chorus: My grace is sufficient for thee
> My grace is sufficient for thee
> Oh! Matchless, boundless grace of God
> My grace is sufficient for thee.
> (Grace Sufficient for Thee by C. M. Robinson)

Are you a fallen Samson already grinding in the enemy's prison? Your hair will surely grow again. Don't give up, rise up, make your peace with God, break the enemy's chains, and move forward. His grace is sufficient for you.

CHAPTER 10

Proud Nebuchadnezzar Ate Grass

Nebuchadnezzar was a Babylonian king who militarily bestrode the world around him like a mighty colossus, ruling over a huge economically powerful empire. He conquered Jerusalem and took away not only goods, including temple cups, but also many youths, including Daniel, Meshack, Shadrack, and Abednigo.

> In the third year of the reign of Jehoiakim king of Judah came Nebuchadnezzar king of Babylon into Jerusalem, and besieged it. And the Lord gave Jehoiakim king of Judah into his hand, with part of the vessels of the house of God: which he carried into the land of Shinar to the house of his god; and he brought the vessels into the treasure house of his god. And the king spake unto Ashpenaz the master of his eunuchs, that he should bring certain of the children of Israel, and of the king's seed, and of the princes; Children in whom was no blemish, but well favoured, and skilful in all wisdom, and cunning in knowledge, and understanding science, and such as had ability in them to stand in the king's palace, and whom they might teach the learning and the tongue of the Chaldeans. And the king appointed them a daily provision of the king's meat, and of the wine which he drank: so nourishing them three years, that at the end thereof they might stand before the king. Now among these were of the children of Judah, Daniel, Hananiah, Mishael, and Azariah. (Dan. 1:1–6)

Nebuchadnezzar had a dream

He later had a dream which greatly troubled him, especially since he could not even recall the details. All his astrologers failed in their attempt to solve the riddle. They finally called Daniel who not only told the king his dream, but also interpreted it.

Shocked at the level of Daniel's wisdom, the king stood up from the throne and publicly bowed down and worshipped Daniel, pronouncing Daniel's "God as the God of all gods" (Dan. 2:46–49). He also promoted him and his friends.

A golden image

Having made a public pronouncement that Daniel's God is the God of all gods, you would have expected that Nebuchadnezzar converted. The way we celebrate mere statements of piety of some leaders and celebrities even when they remained, unconverted is troubling to discerning minds but instead, Nebuchadnezzar accepted advice from flatterers, made a large golden image, and ordered everyone to worship it. Whoever refused was to be thrown into the furnace of fire (Dan. 3:1–4). When Meshack, Shadrack, and Abednigo, Daniel's friends refused to bow to his image, they were thrown into the fiery furnace, but they were not burnt. Instead, a forth heavenly being joined them in the fire (Dan. 3:13–25).

Royal decree to worship God Almighty

Shocked at the miraculous preservation that was displayed right before him, the king decreed that only the God of Meshack, Shadrack, and Abednigo was to be worshipped, and that whoever worshipped another god would be cut into pieces and his house reduced to a dunghill.

> Then Nebuchadnezzar came near to the mouth of the burning fiery furnace, and spake, and said, Shadrach, Meshach, and Abednego, ye servants of the most high God, come forth, and come hither, then Shadrach, Meshach, and Abednego, came forth of the midst of the fire. And the princes, governors, and captains, and the king's counsellors, being gathered together, saw these men, upon whose bodies the fire had no power, nor was

an hair of their head singed, neither were their coats changed, nor the smell of fire had passed on them. Then Nebuchadnezzar spake, and said, Blessed be the God of Shadrach, Meshach, and Abednego, who hath sent his angel, and delivered his servants that trusted in him, and have changed the king's word, and yielded their bodies, that they might not serve nor worship any god, except their own God. Therefore I make a decree, That every people, nation, and language, which speak anything amiss against the God of Shadrach, Meshach, and Abednego, shall be cut in pieces, and their houses shall be made a dunghill: because there is no other God that can deliver after this sort. Then the king promoted Shadrach, Meshach, and Abednego, in the province of Babylon. (Dan. 3:26–30)

Nebuchadnezzar promoted the three Hebrews to high positions within his kingdom. One would have thought he had learned his lesson and converted to the worship of the only true God Almighty. Even his own decree was not strong enough to compel him to worship God.

Another dream

It was business as usual for the king till he had another dream in which he saw a big tree that served as a shade and food for many people and even animals, "a holy one" came down from heaven to give an order that the tree be cut down leaving only the stump (Dan. 4:10–17). As usual, after all the court magicians failed, Daniel was called in to interpret the dream. He told the king that the tree represented him, and God had decreed he would be driven out his kingdom to live and eat grass in the bush for seven years in harsh weather till he acknowledged God as the one who rules in the kingdom of men and gives power to whoever he chooses. Moreover, the stump was to be left so that he might still return after having learned his lesson.

> The tree that thou sawest, which grew, and was strong, whose height reached unto the heaven, and the sight thereof to all the earth; Whose leaves were fair, and the fruit thereof much, and in it was meat for all; under which the beasts of the field dwelt, and upon whose branches the fowls of the heaven had their habitation: It is thou, O king, that art grown and become strong: for thy greatness is grown, and reacheth unto heaven, and thy dominion to the end of the earth. And whereas the king saw a watcher and an holy one coming down from heaven, and saying, Hew the tree down, and destroy it; yet leave the stump of the roots thereof in the earth, even with a band of iron and brass, in the tender grass of the field; and let it be wet with the dew of heaven, and let his portion be with the beasts of the field, till seven times pass over him; This is the interpretation, O king, and this is the decree of the most High, which is come upon my lord the king: That they shall drive thee from men, and thy dwelling shall be with the beasts of the field, and they shall make thee to eat grass as oxen, and they shall wet thee with the dew of heaven, and seven times shall pass over thee, till thou know that the most High ruleth in the kingdom of men, and giveth it to whomsoever he will. And whereas they commanded to leave the stump of the tree roots; thy kingdom shall be sure unto thee, after that thou shalt have known that the heavens do rule. (Dan. 4:20–26)

Daniel advised him to repent of his sins and live in righteousness so that God could have mercy on him (Dan. 4:27).

The axe falls

However sobering and scary such news would be to a reasonable man, it was not strong enough to drive him to God, not this proud king. He continued life as usual till one day after twelve full months, he walked through his palace, boasting and congratulating himself for having built the great Babylon by the might of his own power for the honor of his majesty (Dan. 4:29–30).

This was the last straw. God had had enough, so He called from heaven and dissolved his government, declaring that he would be driven to the bush to eat grass like the oxen till he acknowledged God as the most high God, ruler in the kingdom of men (Dan. 4:31–32). The same hour, all the decrees of God came to pass. His subjects drove him away, he ate grass, and his hair grew like an eagle's feathers and his nails like bird's claws under the harsh weather (without a shelter), roaming the bush in the midst of animals (Dan. 4:33). I am sure the gorillas and monkeys would have accepted him as one of them or taunted him for his predicament for seven years.

Restored upon repentance

When the seven years had passed, Nebuchadnezzar repented and gave all glory to God whom he now recognized as the God who liveth forever and whose kingdom is forever. He also acknowledged that those who walk in pride, God is able to abase (Dan. 4:34–37). From his story, you can see God restored him and his kingdom. This is a lesson for those in political or other high positions that they should be careful how they use their privileged position. They should rule with the fear of God.

Lessons

i. Acknowledge God in all your ways, never think your strength or power alone made you get to where you are or accomplish whatever achievements you made today or in the future. I usually shake my head when I hear people claim they achieved some things by "dint of hard work." Never let your heart become boastful for anything you achieved, let alone against your Maker who sustains your very life.

ii. Whenever God grants you the privilege of being warned to desist from sin, don't even wait till the evening prayer time before you repent. Nebuchadnezzar had twelve months notice of the impending catastrophe, but he ignored the warning and paid dearly for it. Even though he was restored, I am sure his experience in the bush would have been an indelible memory till he died. The memories would have kept him in check for the rest of his life.

CHAPTER 11

Belshazzar Saw the Handwriting on the Wall

Belshazzar, the son of Nebuchadnezzar, who ought to have learned lessons of life from the historical experience of his father's humiliation and exaltation by God, never did. Instead, he lived as if there was no God anywhere.

One day, he threw a party for about one thousand guests, his nobles, wives, and concubines. After drinking wine and probably getting a little bit drunk, he remembered the gold cups his father had taken from the Jerusalem temple when he had conquered them. He called for them, and they used these consecrated cups to drink. As if this affront to the living God was not bad enough, they started singing praises to their gods of gold, silver, bronze, iron, wood, and stone.

> Belshazzar the king made a great feast to a thousand of his lords, and drank wine before the thousand. Belshazzar, whiles he tasted the wine, commanded to bring the golden and silver vessels which his father Nebuchadnezzar had taken out of the temple which was in Jerusalem; that the king, and his princes, his wives, and his concubines, might drink therein. Then they brought the golden vessels that were taken out of the temple of the house of God which was at Jerusalem; and the king, and his princes, his wives, and his concubines, drank in them. They drank wine, and praised the gods of gold, and of silver, of brass, of iron, of wood, and of stone. (Dan. 5:1–4)

Praising idols while drinking from God's holy vessels was an affront to God. Swiftly, God gave him and his vile government summary trial in heaven and wrote the judgment in heavenly language. To add a touch of drama and show the fierceness of God's anger, God made a visible heavenly hand write the judgment on in wall, making it also visible to all present (Dan. 5:5). This is where the popular term "he should have seen the handwriting on the wall" comes from.

The king is frightened

The king became so frightened that he started shaking his knees knocking against each other, giving way (Dan. 5:6). Such disgrace was not common. Kings were supposed to be bold and never show any sign of fear publicly, but this time, Belshazzar could not but show fright publicly.

Astrology failed the king

As many people often do in times of crisis, the first people he called were his official astrologers, sorcerers, and various occultists to help interpret the writing on the wall. Not even the promise of great rewards that included the third highest position in the kingdom could produce results; all of them failed woefully. The king became more subdued and frightened with his nobles speechless (Dan. 5:7–8). This is one of the reasons I pity all unbelievers who still trust soothsayers, occultists, and other satanic sources for solutions to problems that should be placed at the feet of our ever-living Jesus Christ. They often discover to their chagrin that these agents of the devil can only add to their problems.

Daniel comes to judgment

Daniel's gift brought him before the king once again, having been introduced by the queen, expatiating on his exploits during Nebuchadnezzar's reign.

Desperate for a solution, Belshazzar offered a chain of gold and the third highest position in the land to him, if only he could interpret the writings (Dan. 5:13–16).

Daniel took the king on a historical excursion of how God had dealt with his once proud father and humbled him when his heart was lifted up (Dan. 5:8–22). He further told him he had not humbled himself despite having full knowledge of his father's humiliation. Having lifted up himself against God using God's sanctified vessels to drink wine with his nobles and concubines and praising idols in such revelry, was too much of an affront against the all-powerful God (Dan. 5:22–24).

Interpretation

Daniel gave him the sad meaning of the handwriting (Dan. 5:25–28) with his kingdom pronounced dead and given to the Medes and Persians. Belshazzar, in a show of bravado, still went ahead to promote Daniel the third highest ruler over the Babylonian government which the God of heaven had already pronounced dead. I wonder whether he thought it was all a joke or a bad dream from which he would soon awake (Dan. 5:29).

That very night, Darius the Medo-Persian ruler invaded Babylon, killed Belshazzar, and began to rule over his country (Dan. 5:30).

Lessons

i.   No matter how powerful our position is, we must recognize God as the sovereign Lord over all the affairs of men and humble ourselves before Him.

ii. We must learn the right lesson from the fall of others. Had Belshazzar learned from the bitter experience of his father, he would not have dared God like that.

iii. We must respect whatever belongs to God and not be tempted to use the same for ungodly purposes.

iv. Never let your heart be lifted up against God, neither give praises due to Him to graven images. This always displeases God who will punish promptly.

v.   If someone had gone to the party while the revelry was going on to ask them to stop, the king would likely have promptly ordered the person's execution or imprisonment. How many refuse the voice of men and women of God today till the party suddenly comes to an end for them? You don't tell a deaf person that the market is over; when he does not see anybody again in the market, he will know it's time to close up shop and go home. A word is enough for the wise.

CHAPTER 12

Lucifer Fell to Pride and Unbridled Ambition

L ucifer was an archangel created by God with the most beautiful material anyone can imagine, very rare precious stones of beautiful colors to serve as the heavenly choir leader.

In fact, it is believed that most parts of his body were almost musical in nature.

> Moreover the word of the LORD came unto me, saying, Son of man, take up a lamentation upon the king of Tyrus, and say unto him, Thus saith the Lord God; Thou sealest up the sum, full of wisdom, and perfect in beauty. Thou hast been in Eden the garden of God; every precious stone was thy covering, the sardius, topaz, and the diamond, the beryl, the onyx, and the jasper, the sapphire, the emerald, and the carbuncle, and gold: the workmanship of thy tabrets and of thy pipes was prepared in thee in the day that thou wast created. Thou art the anointed cherub that covereth; and I have set thee so: thou wast upon the holy mountain of God; thou hast walked up and down in the midst of the stones of fire. (Ezek. 28:11–14)

He was perfect in all his ways till iniquity was found in him (Ezek. 28:15). He was expelled from the mount of God because of violence when his heart was lifted up on account of his beauty, and he corrupted his God-given wisdom, having among other things desecrated his sanctuary (Ezek. 28:16–18). Pride means having too high an opinion of one's self-importance or superiority (Prov. 29:23, 16:18, 8:13).

Unbridled ambition

Apart from pride, one of the problems of proud people is inability to know their limits while underestimating others. They are always rating themselves beyond what they truly are, only to find out their true worth or ability when it is too late.

He wanted to be greater than God

Lucifer, at the height of his pride, imagined himself to be capable of making a throne for himself above the stars of God who had created him beautifully to serve Him.

> How art thou fallen from heaven, O Lucifer, son of the morning! how art thou cut down to the ground, which didst weaken the nations! For thou hast said in thine heart, I will ascend into heaven, I will exalt my throne above the stars of God: I will sit also upon the mount of the congregation, in the sides of the north: I will ascend above the heights of the clouds; I will be like the most High. (Isa. 14:12–14)

From the above, it was clear that he was not only interested in a high throne but also wanted to become equal with God, calling the shots like the Almighty as co-governor of the heavens and the earth. What a very tall ambition! Pride would not allow him to admit he was on a suicide mission. He managed to convince one third of the angels of God to follow him in his palace coup against the sovereign God. Needless to say, he lost woefully and was cast down from his heavenly position into the earth (Rev. 12:7–12).

Did music stop in heaven?

If you think sonorous music stopped in heaven because Lucifer the choirmaster was cast out, you cannot be more wrong. Many angels and the saints of God have taken the music department to a level Lucifer could never have imagined. Hallelujah.

How Lucifer will end

For now, God has chosen in His sovereignty to allow Lucifer, now known as Satan, the dragon (and many other names), to continue to move to and from all corners of the earth, deceiving those who will not accept the truth as preached by Jesus Christ and His many ministers on earth. He holds himself up as a very powerful deity worthy of human worship with many lying wonders. When his time is up, just a single angel of God will arrest him and lock him up in a pit for one thousand years (Rev. 20:1–3). During this time, Satan's powerlessness will become apparent to those with discerning minds.

In the final judgment, Satan will be cast out with all those who followed and are still following him into the lake of fire where they will be tormented day and night FOREVER (Rev. 20:7–10).

You have a choice, either to learn from Lucifer's fall and avoid his mistakes or repeat them and share in his final doom. It is my prayer that you will choose the path of life through Jesus Christ, our Lord and Savior (Amen).

CHAPTER 13

Covetousness and Idolatry Destroyed Ahab

T he story of King Ahab, the son of Omri, the seventh king of Israel, is such a sad one that the Bible actually started reporting it with a sad summary of how he married Jezebel who brought so much evil to the land, killed many, and went on to worship Baal.

> And Ahab the son of Omri did evil in the sight of the LORD above all that were before him. And it came to pass, as if it had been a light thing for him to walk in the sins of Jeroboam the son of Nebat, that he took to wife Jezebel the daughter of Ethbaal king of the Zidonians, and went and served Baal, and worshipped him. And he reared up an altar for Baal in the house of Baal, which he had built in Samaria. And Ahab made a grove; and Ahab did more to provoke the LORD God of Israel to anger than all the kings of Israel that were before him. (1 Kings 16:30–33)

The worship of idols more or less became a state religion because of the strong backing of Jezebel's prophets of Baal.

He ignored godly prophets

Ahab not only killed the genuine prophets of God; he ignored the surviving ones, including the great Elijah who could have guided him right with godly counsel.

The neglect was such that Elijah was moved to make a prophetic declaration that there would be no rain over the land for three and half years (1 Kings 17:1). As usual, his prophecy was scorned, and Elijah was ignored by the authorities in power. However, when it became clear that their false prophets could not reverse Elijah's pronouncement, they started looking for Elijah. When Elijah showed up, Ahab accused him of being the one troubling Israel (1 Kings 18:17–18). Elijah pointedly told him he (Ahab) was the one troubling Israel for following Baalim. Elijah threw up the challenge to prove who is God between Baal and God Almighty by determining who would send fire to consume the sacrifice from heaven (1 Kings 18:19–24). Baal's prophets failed to bring any fire but Elijah's God brought fire down to consume the sacrifice soaked with water (a very scarce commodity then) within a very short time (1 Kings 18:30–39). Elijah proceeded to kill all the prophets of Baal, four hundred and fifty in all. If you think Ahab was converted, how wrong can you be? He ran home to tell Jezebel all the feats performed by Elijah and how he (Ahab) watched helplessly as their official "prophets" were being slaughtered (1 Kings 19:11). Jezebel issued a death warrant on Elijah. Elijah, knowing Jezebel's order was as good as law under Ahab's despotic government, took to his heels (1 Kings 19:2).

Ahab covets Naboth's vineyard

Again, Ahab coveted Naboth's vineyard despite his having access to many others as a king. Naboth's refusal to yield led to the king becoming sad and moody in the palace, refusing to eat (1 Kings 21:1–4). Jezebel stepped in, plotted, and killed Naboth to give way to the state acquisition of the private property (1 Kings 21:7–19). They did just that, stoned innocent Naboth to death, and Ahab then proceeded happily to take possession of the vineyard (1 Kings 21:12–16).

God judges Ahab

God of heaven with His all-seeing eye sent Elijah to tell Ahab that the dogs would lick his blood in the same place they had licked that of Naboth (1 Kings 21:17–24). God promised to have dogs eat the body of Jezebel by the wall of Jezreel (Naboth's town, to give her maximum disgrace). God also did not spare all the males in his house but cut off his family prosperity (1 Kings 21:17–24). Again, the Bible gives a summary of God's view of his rules as it did at the beginning of his story (1 Kings 21:25–26).

Ahab becomes sober

For once, Ahab changed his attitude when he heard of the calamity that was to befall him and his family even though he initially regarded Elijah as his enemy (1 Kings 21:20). He tore his dress and wore sackcloth, fasted, and spoke softly (1 Kings 21:27). The compassionate God had pity on him after he humbled himself, postponing the enforcement of some parts of the judgment till the days of his children (1 Kings 21:28–29).

Ahab goes to war

After three years without war between Israel and Syria, one eventually broke out. Prompted by Jehoshaphat, Ahab engaged the services of probably the four hundred Asherah priests left alive by Elijah at Mount Carmel (when he killed the four hundred and fifty prophets of Baal) and pretended to seek the face of God concerning the war. They told him what he wanted to hear: "Go and smite your enemies," they said (1 Kings 22:4–6).

Not satisfied by the prophecies of these "prophets," Jehoshaphat demanded a second consultation of another prophet over the issue (1 Kings 22:7–8). From the above, it is clear that Ahab still disliked any prophet who spoke the truth, but Jehoshaphat, King of Judah, insisted they should call in prophet Micaiah. They tried to put pressure on Micaiah to align himself with the majority prophecies (1 Kings 22:13). Micaiah told them sarcastically to go and prosper and win the ward (Kings 22:14–15). Ahab was happy within himself but pretended to put pressure on Micaiah to speak the true mind of God (1 Kings 22:16).

The bombshell, and Ahab got angry

When prophet Micaiah told Ahab that he saw Israel scattered upon the hills as a sheep without a shepherd, Ahab was furious with him, turned to Jehoshaphat, and asked rhetorically whether he did not tell him before that Micaiah never prophesied anything good concerning him. (1 Kings 22:17–18). All efforts to persuade the king with details of what he saw in the realm of the spirit would not change Ahab's mind.

Ahab imprisoned Micaiah

Ahab ordered Micaiah imprisoned, to be fed half-starved till he came back from the war to decide his fate.

> And the king of Israel said, Take Micaiah, and carry him back unto Amon the governor of the city, and to Joash the king's son; And say, Thus saith the king, Put this fellow in the prison, and feed him with bread of affliction and with water of affliction, until I come in peace. (1 Kings 22:26–27)

Micaiah, being very sure of what God had told him, said if Ahab returned, it would mean that God had not spoken to him (1 Kings 22:28). How many modern-day prophets can stand up to those in power like Micaiah? May God give us prophets who will speak and stand by the word of God at all times in our generation.

Ahab gets killed in war

Against godly counsel, Ahab went to war, but not before convincing Jehoshaphat his visiting friend and King of Judah to dress like himself in kingly robes while Ahab dressed as an ordinary soldier (1 Kings 22:29–30). Unknown to Jehoshaphat, the King of Syria had given orders for his thirty-two captains, leading his army to specifically look out for Ahab and kill him. They almost killed Jehoshaphat before he cried out and they left him alone (1 Kings 22:32–33). A stray arrow not aimed at Ahab directly hit him straight away. He was fatally wounded but stayed in his chariot till the evening when he died (1 Kings 22:34–37).

Dogs feast on Ahab's blood

As they washed the chariot stained with Ahab's blood, the dogs came by divine appointment and licked the blood (1 Kings 22:38), thus fulfilling God's pronouncement on him earlier. Thus came to an end the terrible reign of Ahab over Israel.

Summary

Below is a brief summary of what leads people to discovering that God has replaced them and moved forward with His programs without them. You will do yourself a lot of good to avoid these snares.

1. Pride. God hates pride. In fact, He distances Himself from any proud person but gives grace to the humble. Pride makes people become self-opinionated, incorrigible to the point of resisting wise counsel that would have made them avoid pitfalls. Pride goes before destruction.
2. Avoid allowing even the smallest similitude of an idol to stay in your heart, let alone getting involved with idol worship or occult practices for whatever reason(s).
3. Never consider yourself indispensable to the successful execution of God's program. There are many people who are better than you out there.
4. Flee from sin and humble yourself before God when you are rebuked either by God or through God's servants. Make immediate corrections before God calls in your substitute.
5. Yield promptly to God's call and discharge your responsibilities promptly. Do not wait to serve God with the tail end of your life after being retired by men or corporate organizations which no longer can use you.
6. Do not run the ministry like a personal or family business. Wield the big stick when your family members or anyone for that matter errs. Don't wait till God comes down to do it for you, or the ministry is abandoned by God.

7. Covetousness, envy, over ambition, and personal aggrandizement should not have any place in your life and ministry.

8. Never take God for granted, no matter how close you may seem to God. Moses and Elijah were close, but it did not avail them much when they disappointed God.

9. Say no to any temptation to become a mercenary minister who is ready to do anybody's bidding once the cash or reward is right. Balaam did not find the consequences rewarding.

10. Whatever your achievements are in life, return all the glory to God. Don't turn yourself into a deity or someone who has achieved those feats by dint of your hard work or power. Remember Thomas Andrews who built the famous ship Titanic? He was known to be very particular about details, and as the ship went on its first voyage, he kept on taking notes on what should be improved about the ship. After the construction of the Titanic, a reporter asked Andrews how safe the Titanic would be. With an ironic tone, he said, "Not even God can sink it." We all know what became of the ship. On it's first voyage, it struck an iceberg, and over a thousand people died. Even now, the film Titanic makes people weep when they watch the extent of human and material disaster he brought on so many, including rich and powerful passengers.

11. Obey God's word and instructions to precision in doing His work. You have no opinion or right that qualifies you to modify them. Saul's partial obedience and God's reactions should be a lesson to us.

12. Stop going along with sinful people or servants of God who are living defiantly against God's word, no matter how powerful their positions (political, business, or spiritual) may be. Withdrawing yourself from them like Prophet Samuel did to Saul will help them reflect soberly, rather than giving tacit public or private approval to their evil ways.

God bless you as you reflect on the lessons, and amend your ways where necessary before it is too late. And remember, that God called and invested so much grace in you is a privilege. Never take God for granted. He has better candidates waiting to replace you if you fail Him. May God help us all to be faithful to Him who has called us to the end in Jesus's name (Amen).

About the Author

Patrick Adewale Mould, an accountant and a 1996 graduate of Life Theological Seminary, Ikorodu, Lagos, Nigeria, has been in the ministry as pastor/evangelist for over thirty years, focusing on salvation, healing, and deliverance from demonic oppression.

He founded and pastored Maranatha Royal Church in Lagos, Nigeria, for many years before answering God's call as a missionary evangelist. He is currently based in Toronto, Canada, from where he reaches North America, Europe, and Africa with his life-transforming preaching of God's word and prayers that have brought thousands of souls into God's kingdom.

A revivalist and regular conference speaker, he is married to Pastor (Mrs.) Morolayo Mould, and they are blessed with one daughter, Deborah, and three sons, Daniel, Joshua, and Emmanuel.

Author's contact
Email: patsainternational@yahoo.com
Follow me on facebook.com/adewale.mould

CPSIA information can be obtained
at www.ICGtesting.com
Printed in the USA
LVHW031951151019
634316LV00001B/1/P